JAMESTOWN  PUBLISHERS

W9-AGK-447

FRIGHT WRITE

It's a Mystery to Me

FRIGHT WRITE

A SHOCKINGLY SUPERIOR READING AND WRITING PROGRAM

It's a Mystery to Me

Write Your Own Scary Screenplay

JAMESTOWN ⛵ PUBLISHERS

a division of NTC/CONTEMPORARY PUBLISHING COMPANY
Lincolnwood, Illinois USA

Editorial Director: Cynthia Krejcsi

Executive Editor: Marilyn Cunningham

Editorial Services Manager: Sylvia Bace

Market Development Manager: Mary Sue Dillingofski

Design Manager: Ophelia M. Chambliss

Production and Design: PiperStudiosInc

Cover Composition: Doug Besser

Production Manager: Margo Goia

ISBN: 0-89061-865-8

Published by Jamestown Publishers,

a division of NTC/Contemporary Publishing Company,

4255 West Touhy Avenue,

Lincolnwood (Chicago), Illinois 60646-1975, U.S.A.

Manufactured in the United States of America.

7890 VL 9 8 7 6 5 4 3 2

CONTENTS

The Mystery of Titan   2

Don Wulffson

> Beasts . . . jelly . . . slime. What's happening to the space
> mission on Titan is criminal!

Vanished   8

Q. L. Pearce

> What happened to over 100 English colonists on Roanoke
> Island? It's one of America's great unsolved mysteries.

Foul Play   12

Don Wulffson

> Is this a case of foul play or an innocent accident? You decide.

Screaming at the Wall   21

Neal Shusterman

> Grandma's been acting funny lately. But there's nothing
> funny about what's happening.

Night Rider   32

Scott Ingram

> Rachel has to prove to her parents that she is old enough
> to drive—no matter what!

The Quarterback's Revenge   43

Catherine Gourley

> After twenty years, Altamonte Heights once again has
> a young coach, a talented quarterback, and a winning
> football team. Will history repeat itself?

Hide-and-Seek   57

Allen B. Ury

> Any twelve-year-old can baby-sit a nine-year-old for two
> hours. After all, what could possibly go wrong?

A Grave Mistake   70

Don Wulffson

> Would you take a summer job at a cemetery? Carrie did.

The Great Pyramid at Giza   77

Q. L. Pearce

> It would be difficult to build this enormous pyramid today.
> How did people build it forty-five centuries ago?

The Mystery of the *Mary Celeste*   81

Don Wulffson

> A century ago, the entire crew of the *Mary Celeste* vanished.
> Could a newly found diary solve the mystery?

Ancient Maps   88

Q. L. Pearce

> If Columbus didn't discover the New World, then who did?

A Case of Being Yourself   92

Don Wulffson

> A girl has been kidnapped. Are you up to solving the case?

By the Book   114

Don Wulffson

> Melissa has written many unpublished murder mysteries.
> But she's positive she can sell her new manuscript.

To the Reader

READ AT YOUR OWN RISK

Don't you love a good mystery? There's nothing like a rotting corpse, sinister suspects, and deadly deceptions to get the day going. We'll let you know right now—it was *not* Colonel Mustard in the library with a wrench. Still clueless? You won't be for long.

This book will also help you solve one of the great mysteries of our time—how you can become a shockingly superior writer. See how professional writers keep their characters in character and build suspense. Find out how to foreshadow events and bury important clues. Learn how to present a chilling story that will puzzle and perplex. Learn how to **FRIGHT WRITE!**

The Mystery of Titan

What's happening to the colonists on Titan?
So far, no one has a clue.

What do you think a di-trobe dome might look like?

transmission: a message sent through space by radio waves

Tanya Ling was extremely proud of her dad. He had verified that Titan, the largest and brightest of Saturn's ten satellites, possessed an atmosphere. Then, using unmanned space probes, he determined that Titan's atmosphere could sustain human life and that the satellite was rich in zinium, a metal far stronger and, in many ways, more precious than diamonds. Finally, it had been her father's concept, his vision, to send settlers to Titan, to colonize the satellite and begin mining operations there.

All had been going well. Thirty-one colonists had set up a di-trobe dome in which to live. Mining had begun. Unmanned space freighters had been readied to carry the precious cargo to Earth. The colonists had reported no problems. Then suddenly a disturbing <u>transmission</u> came. It was garbled, distorted, and frightening. Tanya remembered listening to her dad, in his study, playing a recording of the transmission over and over: "Beasts . . . everywhere . . . jelly . . . slime . . . kill us!" There had been no further transmissions from Titan ever since.

"It's obvious, honey," Edward Ling had confided to his daughter, "that there are living creatures on Titan. Apparently they have killed the colonists. But we're not beaten yet!"

It took only two months to get a second manned flight to Titan funded and under way. This time fifty-four soldiers armed with the latest weaponry were sent to the satellite. Their goal: to find any survivors and to wipe out the beasts on Titan.

The flight went well. Upon landing, the soldiers found the colony all but destroyed. The dome, where the colonists had lived, and the mines, where they had worked, were in a shambles. Not a single surviving colonist was found, nor were any remains. But the soldiers did find the beasts of Titan—red, slimy, jellylike creatures, which undoubtedly had killed and eaten the humans.

Day after day the soldiers engaged the horrible creatures in battle. The body count was transmitted back to Earth from the colonel in charge. On day one he reported six beasts killed; day two, seven killed; day three, eleven killed and four wounded; day four, two killed and one wounded. On the fifth day, and thereafter, the colonel reported that there were no further contacts with the enemy. Possibly all had been killed; or, more probably, the rest had withdrawn and were in hiding. The only other occurrence of note was that the wounded beasts, all five of them, had died in captivity. Like the other dead, they were all <u>cremated</u>.

More than half the soldiers were set to work mining, while the others stood guard or scouted the satellite for more of the beasts. Zinium ore was hacked and drilled,

cremated: burned to ashes

How many beasts were killed or died in captivity?

PREDICT

What do you think is happening to the colonists? Could their headaches and rashes mean anything?

How many aliens were killed by the third contingent of soldiers?

incomprehensible: impossible to understand

contingent: a group that is part of a larger group

subsequently: later

expeditionary: on a trip made for a special purpose, such as exploring a new territory

graded, and readied for transport to Earth. Transmissions to Earth were clear and on schedule, and there were no reports of any unusual problems . . . except that some of the soldiers complained of headaches, rashes, and homesickness. All seemed to be going well.

And then the transmissions stopped again.

For two days, ground control frantically tried to make contact. Not until late on the third day were the soldiers heard from. The transmission was as shocking, disturbing, and <u>incomprehensible</u> as the one sent by the first group of colonists: "Everywhere slime . . . eat flesh . . . brains . . . no stopping . . . too fast . . . !" After that, nothing but silence.

A third <u>contingent</u> of soldiers, one hundred strong, was sent to Titan to find out what happened and to rescue any survivors. They killed thirty-nine aliens, wounded nine, and captured six. As before, all the wounded and captured also <u>subsequently</u> died and were cremated. As for the soldiers of the third contingent, there was not a single casualty.

But the sigh of relief on Earth did not last long. Shortly thereafter, a garbled transmission—similar to the ones sent by the first two contingents—came, followed by complete silence.

When her father came home from work each day, Tanya could see the strain increasing on his face. Neither he nor anyone else had been able to figure out what was wiping out the colonists, the force of fifty-four well-armed soldiers that followed, or the most recent <u>expeditionary</u> force of soldiers. What had they been up against? What had attacked them? What sort of horrid battles had they fought . . . and finally lost?

In short, what was the solution to the riddle of Titan?
An answer had to be found.

"The only way we can find out what happens up there," Edward Ling told his daughter one day after work, "is to send another—even larger—force to Titan. In fact, today we received presidential approval for a force of five thousand more troops."

That night, Edward Ling went to bed early. Unable to sleep, Tanya went to her dad's study. She listened to recordings, studied computer printouts, and pored over facts, figures, names, and dates. She was bleary-eyed, exhausted, and it was almost morning when she saw it. She stared in shock; it—the answer—was right there in front of her. And it was all so simple.

"I've got it!" she exclaimed, rushing into her father's bedroom and shaking him awake.

"Got what?" he asked drowsily, yawning.

"The answer to what happens on Titan—the solution to the mystery!"

Mr. Ling sat up and stared at his daughter.

"It's mostly a question of numbers," said Tanya, a calculator in one hand and a sheaf of papers in the other.

Her father gave her a puzzled look, then nodded, gesturing for her to continue.

"How many settlers were in the first colony?" she asked.

"Thirty-one."

"And how many in the second flight—the military expedition?"

Stop reading. Can you find the answer before Tanya provides it? What is the solution? Explain your answer.

"Fifty-four."

"Do you know what I'm getting at?" asked Tanya.

"I haven't got a clue," her father said.

Tanya sat down on the bed. "We lost a total of eighty-five people in the first two expeditions. Compare that with the body count—the total of jellylike aliens killed by our forces. Eighty-five! The exact same number! Do you see now what I'm telling you, Dad?"

"I'm starting to. And it's scaring the devil out of me!"

Tanya continued. "The people complained of headaches and rashes—then something suddenly happened up there. There were the same strange transmissions, as though the senders had all but lost their minds, and then no transmissions at all. Something happens—something sudden—in that place, on that satellite. I don't know exactly what. But they change—humans change into jellylike blobs."

"Which means," said Edward Ling, "that each time we've gone up there to kill aliens, what we've really been killing is our own people—who have <u>mutated</u> into monsters!" He frowned. "Why, their brains must have been <u>deteriorating</u> as rapidly as their bodies—before they could communicate in an understandable way what had happened to them!"

"I think you're right, Dad," said Tanya. "But what do you think caused the mutation?"

"Exposure to zinium, possibly. However, we'll probably never know for sure." He sighed. "Regardless of the cause, one thing we do know is that the same thing has

mutated: changed

deteriorating: becoming worse

happened—or is happening—to the last group of a hundred soldiers sent to Titan. And there's nothing we can do to save them."

"But there is something we can do to save the five thousand soldiers getting ready to go to Titan," said Tanya.

Edward Ling was on the phone almost instantly. Tanya sat quietly and listened as her father explained the solution to the puzzle of Titan to the president.

"So you see, sir," her father concluded, "no further missions should be sent to Titan, nor should any zinium ever be brought to Earth." Then he told the president who had solved the riddle. Smiling, Edward Ling held out the phone to his daughter. "Tanya," he said, "someone would like to speak to you."

Vanished

Four hundred years ago, settling the New World was as strange and mysterious as settling Titan is today.

In the late 1500s, Sir Walter Raleigh of England attempted to establish a British colony on Roanoke Island in North Carolina. Because of the harsh conditions, the first settlement was unsuccessful, and the colonists returned to England. Another small group, also under Raleigh and the British crown, was killed by hostile Indians. In 1587, 112 colonists arrived and established a small village. The group worked hard to build shelters and prepare for the upcoming winter. In August, their leader, John White, sailed to England for more supplies with a crew of fifteen men. He intended to return in the spring, but England and Spain went to war, which prevented White from sailing back to Roanoke until 1590, three years later.

When he finally landed on the tiny island, White found the colony eerily quiet. The ruins of a hastily built fortress and a few other dwellings still stood, but the only trace of the colonists was a single clue: The word CROATOAN had been carved in a doorpost. As soon as possible, an expedition was formed to go to nearby Croatoan Island, home of the Hatteras Indians. That expedition (and the four that followed) failed to turn up the missing colonists. In 1603, the search was abandoned, and the fate of the colonists remains a mystery to this day. Some people say that perhaps they made a new life for themselves and did not want to be found.

• • ● • •

The word CROATOAN carved in a doorpost was perhaps the only clue to the mysterious disappearance of 112 English settlers on Roanoke Island.

• • ● • •

In the eighteenth century, however, settlers along the Lumber River in North Carolina came in contact with a group of Native Americans, the Lumbee of Robeson County, who spoke a language remarkably similar in many ways to English. Although Native Americans generally have dark hair, eyes, and complexions, many Lumbee Indians have light hair and eyes and fair complexions.

It seems that in about 1650, many of the Hatteras tribe of Croatoan moved to the Lumber River Valley on the mainland of North Carolina. They were the ancestors of the current Lumbee Indians. Of the 95 surnames listed for the colonists at Roanoke, 41 are surnames of members of the Lumbee Tribe. Some people think that many of the Lumbee may be descendants of the English colonists who disappeared in 1590.

surnames: family names; last names

Without a Trace

Roanoke isn't the only case of an entire village of people suddenly disappearing. Joe Labelle, a trapper, was not prepared for what greeted him when he visited a tiny village beside Lake Anjikuni in Canada. It was a frigid day in November 1930, and Joe expected most of the 30 inhabitants to be in their huts. Instead, he found everything abandoned, as if the villagers had left quite suddenly. Left behind were food, clothes, guns, and, sadly, seven dogs tethered to a tree stump, dead from starvation. The only thing that appeared to have been taken was a body that had been carefully removed from its grave. Where did the villagers go, and why? No one knows.

The Mystery of Titan

▼ Learning from the Story

Actual events in the news can inspire writers. Think about what event might have given the author the idea for "The Mystery of Titan." Working with several other students, look through a newspaper for an intriguing story. Then play "What If?" with the article. Change something about it to make it a mystery. For example, for a science article about health risks associated with a new wonder drug, you might start by asking, "*What if* someone died from the drug?" Someone adds, "*What if* dozens of people die from the drug?" You suggest, "*What if* the drug company knew about the deadly side effects all along? *What if* there was a massive cover-up?" Play around with the news story until you have the makings of a great mystery.

▼ Putting It into Practice

To get ideas for your own mystery, you might look through a recent newspaper. Clip two or three stories that could become an interesting mystery. Make a list of your story ideas. Don't hesitate to combine pieces of several stories or to change a story around until you come up with the perfect mystery.

FOUL PLAY

WE HAVE A BODY.

WE HAVE A WEAPON.

WE HAVE A SUSPECT.

BUT DO WE HAVE A MURDER?

Shawn Peake was in the front hallway, about to leave for school, when the phone rang. He heard his mom pick it up in the kitchen. There was a short conversation, and then he heard his dad ask, "Who was that?"

"My brother Irving," answered Shawn's mom. "He said he broke his reading glasses. He left his other pair here last Tuesday night and he wondered if Shawn would—"

"Bring them over to him," Shawn said, walking into the kitchen and finishing her sentence. "No problem, Mom. It's on my way to school." He glanced at his watch. "But I'd better get moving. It's already seven-twenty, and I don't want to be late for first period—again!"

"Hold on just a second," said his mom, going into the other room and returning with a box of bandages. "Take these to him, too. He said he cut himself and is all out." She handed Shawn the bandages. "Oh, yes. And he said that if you ring the bell and no one answers, just leave the glasses and the bandages in the mailbox."

Taking the bandages from his mom, along with the pair of glasses she retrieved from the kitchen drawer, Shawn left with an over-the-shoulder "see ya" and headed for the house his two uncles—Doug and Irving Blair—shared. Pulling his parka tight against the cold, he made a silent wish that his uncle Irving wouldn't be there. The man was just plain mean, and Shawn didn't want to see him.

Shawn was crazy about his uncle Doug, though. Like Shawn, he was a baseball fanatic, and even coached Shawn's Little League team. In fact, Doug was really just a big kid himself, trading baseball cards and collecting all sorts of baseball memorabilia—from team pennants to bats and balls signed by some of the more famous players. Of course, it was a little easier for Doug to acquire all this stuff, since he and Irving were co-owners of Blair Sporting Goods.

When Shawn's grandfather died, long before Shawn was even born, he left his daughter, Shawn's mom, a large sum of money and left his sons a house and his business. It was his hope that, by living and working together, the brothers, who had a history of feuding, would grow closer.

But things hadn't exactly turned out that way. Selfish, pudgy, lazy Irving wanted to sell the store and the house, while good-natured Doug refused. A terrible rift grew between the brothers from this and countless other disagreements, until the two were barely speaking. They continued to work together in the store and to live in the same house—Doug at one end of the large two-story, and

parka: a warm jacket with a hood

memorabilia: objects that bring back memories

rift: a split or break

Irving at the other—and though the arrangement was uncomfortable, it appeared to be working.

As Shawn rounded the corner and headed up Hudson Street, where his uncles lived, he glanced at his watch. It was already 7:45. *Now I'll be late for sure!* he told himself, quickening his pace and hurrying up to their front door. He contemplated just tossing the glasses and bandages in the mailbox, then decided to ring the bell. A few moments later, the door suddenly burst open.

"Shawn!" his uncle Doug exclaimed, his face red and frightened looking. "There's been a terrible accident!" He pointed upstairs. "Hurry!" he cried.

"What happened?" Shawn asked, but seeing that his uncle seemed almost in a state of shock, he brushed past him and bounded up the stairs, Doug close on his heels. As he got to the top of the second-floor landing, he noticed the smell of burning wood and, at his feet, saw tiny drops of blood. He followed the drops down the hall, then across the carpet of Irving's bedroom and into the adjoining bathroom. And there, lying on the floor, covered with a towel, was his uncle Irving, his head dripping with blood.

"Call an ambulance!" Shawn yelled at Doug. But already he could see it was too late. Irving had a terrible lump on his forehead and his eyes were glazed over. Clearly, he was dead.

His senses reeling, Shawn knelt down and picked up his uncle's left hand. It was cool to the touch, and the skin was wrinkled from being submerged in water. On the back of Irving's left arm was a deep gash. "How did this happen?" asked Shawn, looking over his shoulder at his now-trembling uncle.

"I'd been out walking," his uncle Doug explained. "On my way upstairs I called Irving's name, and when he didn't answer, I went into his room . . . and then into the bathroom. That's when I found him, lying facedown in the bathtub. Apparently he fell, knocked himself out, and drowned." The poor man burst into tears. "I—I pulled him out of the water . . . and then you showed up."

"We should call my parents," said Shawn. "And the police. What if, while you were out, he was murdered?"

Shawn's uncle grimaced. "I—I suppose you're right," he stammered. "I'll go make the calls." And with that, he hurried from the bathroom.

Shawn studied the area around the body. Bloody tissues overflowed from a wastebasket. On the sink counter were tweezers and a bloody splinter of wood along with one end of the shower curtain rod. Ointments, a bottle of <u>antiseptic</u>, and a clock radio lay on the floor, as though they'd been knocked off the counter by the rod. The clock radio was unplugged, and the hands were stopped at 7:25.

"The ambulance and police are on their way," Doug called from Irving's room, where he'd made the calls. "Your parents are coming, too." He paused for a moment. "Uh, I'd like to be alone for a while, so I think I'll just sit downstairs and wait for them, okay?"

Shawn emerged from the bathroom. "Sure, Uncle Doug. I understand. I'll just stay up here and look around a bit."

Do you believe Doug's story? Why or why not?

antiseptic: a germ-fighting substance

As Doug went downstairs, Shawn headed down the hall, following the scent of burning wood. Entering Doug's bedroom, he went directly to the fireplace, where he saw that the gas log-lighter was on, its flames licking at the remains of a piece of wood. Bending down to get a closer look, Shawn was surprised to see that the wood was the handle of a shattered baseball bat.

"Shawn, where are you?" he heard Doug call.

"In here," Shawn answered, turning off the log-lighter, then rising to his feet.

"Why are you in here?" asked Doug as he entered the bedroom, his eyes darting from his nephew to the fireplace.

Shawn said nothing. He was looking at a deep dent in the plaster of one wall, and at the carpeting below, where splinters of wood lay. He examined them, then made his way to Doug's prized collection of bats. There had been five, but now there were only four. Missing from the bottom pegs was the autographed Hank Aaron bat that his uncle Doug had shown Shawn countless times. He turned around and faced his uncle.

"What really happened, Uncle Doug?" asked Shawn. "Uncle Irving didn't drown, did he?"

"We had a fight," said Doug <u>apprehensively</u>. "But I—"

The sound of approaching sirens interrupted him. Doug turned abruptly and headed downstairs. "We'll talk later, Shawn," he said over his shoulder. And a moment later he was opening the door for the paramedics and police officers.

"The body's upstairs," Doug said grimly. Then he went into the living room and sat dejectedly on the sofa.

Why do you think Doug was trying to burn the baseball bat?

apprehensively:
fearfully

The <u>coroner</u> arrived about five minutes later, followed by Shawn's parents. As the police trooped through the house, looking for signs of foul play, Shawn's parents talked to his uncle.

"I can't believe this is happening," Shawn's uncle said to his weeping sister. "First I had yet another fight with Irving. Then I went for a walk, and I came home to find him dead." He looked at a policeman dusting for fingerprints. "And now everybody thinks I'm a murderer!" He smiled grimly, then pulled a slip of paper from his pocket. "Actually, this is my second brush with the law today. Look at this," he said, tossing the paper on the coffee table. "I got a ticket for <u>jaywalking</u> over on Claremont when I went for a walk earlier."

Shawn picked up the ticket and was examining it when a heavyset detective and two uniformed officers suddenly entered the room.

"It's pretty clear what happened," said the detective to Doug. "You fought with your brother, hit him with the bat, then dragged the body to his bathroom. Then you filled the tub and tried to make it look as though he'd fallen and drowned. I'm sorry, sir, but you didn't do a very good cover-up job."

"No!" exclaimed Doug. "That's not what happened. The only part you have right is that we had a fight." He turned to his sister. "It was about selling the store again, but this time it got out of hand. Irving grabbed my Hank Aaron bat and took a swing at me. He missed and hit the wall, breaking the bat."

PREDICT

How could this ticket turn out to be important? What makes you think as you do?

coroner: a public official who examines bodies to investigate the cause of death

jaywalking: crossing a street illegally

"If, supposedly, your brother came after you with the bat, then why did you try to burn it?" asked the officer, holding up the charred handle.

"Because I knew how bad it would look," said Doug. "The bat had his blood on it. When it shattered, a splinter went into his arm. He went to his room, and I was so upset, I went for a walk. When I came back, I—I found him lying dead in the tub."

The detective frowned. "That's your story?" he scoffed as he pulled handcuffs from his belt. "Mr. Blair, I'm afraid I'm going to have to place you under arrest for the murder of—"

"No!" blurted Shawn. "My uncle's telling the truth. It was an accident, and I can prove it!"

The detective frowned. "All right, I'm listening."

"First," said Shawn, "Uncle Doug would never have used one of his bats as a weapon. And especially not his Hank Aaron bat. It was his most prized possession."

"I hope you've got more than that, son," the detective said impatiently.

"A lot more," said Shawn. "At seven-fifteen, my uncle Irving called our house and asked for his glasses and bandages. That means that the fight and his injury had already occurred by then. But even more important is the fact that he said to just leave the stuff in the mailbox if no one answered the door."

"That is what Irving told me," said Shawn's mom.

"I'm not sure I see the <u>significance</u>," said his dad.

"What it means," said Shawn, "is that Uncle Irving was getting ready to take a bath and knew he wouldn't be able

PREDICT

Stop reading. Use the evidence you have to explain what really happened to Uncle Irving.

significance: importance

to answer the door when I arrived. And Uncle Doug wouldn't either because, as Uncle Irving knew, Uncle Doug wasn't home! He was already off on his walk."

"How do we know he didn't come back from his walk," asked the detective, "then enter the house and kill Irving?"

Shawn smiled. "Because, as I'm sure you've figured out, seven twenty-five is the time of death. That's when Uncle Irving, as he fell, tore the shower curtain down, and the rod knocked over the clock radio, stopping the time at seven twenty-five."

"Agreed," said the detective. "We have pinpointed the time of death. But that still doesn't prove Doug wasn't in the house."

"But this does!" exclaimed Shawn, holding up the ticket. "My uncle got a jaywalking ticket on Claremont, which is several blocks from here. And the time on the ticket is seven twenty-six!"

The detective took the ticket from Shawn and examined it. "Well, Mr. Blair," he said, addressing Doug, "it looks to me as though you're guilty . . . of jaywalking, not murder. And it looks to me as though you've got one very fine, very smart nephew."

"Yeah, I think I'll keep him!" said Doug, grinning broadly as he put his arm around Shawn. "I wasn't happy about getting that ticket, but now I think I'll keep it, too!"

FOUL PLAY

▼ Learning from the Story

Shawn cleared his uncle Doug of murder. But he may not have solved the case. Who do you think really killed Uncle Irving? Was his death a case of murder? Working with several other students, try to come up with another ending for "Foul Play." Sketch out the plot and identify the real cause of death.

▼ Putting It into Practice

Before you start writing your own mystery, it's important to think through the crime. Fold a piece of paper into four equal sections. Label the sections Crime, Victim, Suspects/Motives, and Clues. Start thinking through exactly what happened. Name the victim. List possible suspects. As you start fleshing out the story in your mind, you can describe the victim in greater detail, come up with a motive for each suspect, and start listing clues that will help you (and your readers) solve the case.

SCREAMING AT THE WALL

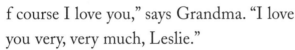

"Of course I love you," says Grandma. "I love you very, very much, Leslie."

Grandma stands inches away from the hallway wall. There is not so much as a picture on the wall, just white paint.

I can see her from my room. The way she stands there talking to the wall—it scares me.

"Let me give you a hug," says Grandma. She holds out her arm and grasps the air in front of her, as if she is hugging someone. But no one is there.

She's been talking to that wall for about a month now. It's not just the wall, though. She'll laugh at some joke that no one except her hears. She'll get angry at someone who's not even in the room. And she treats all of us as if we're invisible.

Dad hardly seems to notice anymore. He's too busy remodeling the house, even late at night. Each night I go to sleep to the sound of saws and hammers and drills.

Mom sits on the edge of my bed, and we talk about things. Lately, we just talk about Grandma.

Some older people live in the past. But Leslie's grandmother seems to live in a completely different world.

"Sometimes it happens like that when you get old. People just sort of wind down," Mom tells me. "It's a part of life."

I think about that: *winding down*, like old gears . . . like our grandfather clock in the hall, which can never keep the right time. But Grandma's not a machine; she's a human being.

I think back to the times when Grandma was okay, before her mind started to slip. She was wonderful and warm and loving. She would take me to the movies and we would talk like the best of friends. But that was a long time ago. Now she's very different. My friends laugh at her, but there's nothing funny about it.

I hear a hammer banging away in the garage. In the kitchen, Grandma sits in the dark. I can hear her talking about the ice cream she's pretending to eat, and then she sings "Happy Birthday" to the empty room. I remember that my birthday is coming up next month.

"That's all right, honey," she says to the dark, empty room. "I don't mind wearing a party hat."

"Who is she talking to?" I ask Mom. "What is she seeing?"

"I don't think we'll ever know," says Mom.

I know what my birthday wish will be. I'll wish that Grandma had her mind back.

It is midnight. I hear Grandma. I leave my room and go into the living room, where Grandma sits in the green velvet chair, watching TV by moonlight. But the TV isn't on.

"They call this music?" she says. "A lot of noise if you ask me. And look at them—grown men with pink hair."

She reaches down beside her and moves her hand back and forth. It takes me a moment to figure out what she's doing. She's petting a dog. But we don't have a dog.

"And what's the point of smashing the guitars?" she says, pointing at the dark TV. "This isn't music; it's a circus."

"Grandma, can you hear me?" I ask.

She looks through me as if I'm not even there. Then, suddenly, she gasps in shock and jumps to her feet. She feels around for the walls as if she's blind.

"I'll go get candles," she says, and then shakes her head with a sigh.

"All this rain," she says. "I've never seen it rain like this." But outside the stars are out and the moon is bright. It isn't raining—not a drop.

What is Grandma talking about? Describe what she seems to be seeing.

Dad works hard every weekend, building our new family room. He pretends that nothing is happening. Grandma is his mother; it must be hard for him to see her like this. I bet he wonders if it will happen to him.

Anyway, he doesn't like to talk about it, but I keep asking because I want answers. I miss the way Grandma used to be.

"It started about five years ago," Dad finally says, resting from his work and drinking a soda. "I remember, I first noticed something was wrong when she started laughing at a joke before the punch line. She just walked away, not even hearing the rest of the joke. Then she would start waking up at all hours of the night. She would go and make herself breakfast and talk at the breakfast table as if we were all there." He shook his head. "It was two o'clock in the morning. Anyway, pretty soon she was living in a whole different world from us."

Dad wipes the sweat from his brow. "She needs us to take care of her now. Okay, Leslie?"

I nod quietly, sorry I made him talk about it.

Dad goes back to his work, burying himself in the room he's adding on, trying not to think about Grandma. I watch as he takes a heavy sledgehammer and swings it at the hall wall, over and over, creating a huge hole that will become the doorway to our new family room.

One night before the family room is finished, Grandma starts screaming at the wall again.

"How dare you!" she screams. "I'm your own flesh and blood!"

The others race in to find her standing in the unfinished family room. "You're going to put me in a <u>sanitarium</u>?" she screams at the <u>drywall</u> in the corner. "That's what you're going to do? I'm not crazy!"

"I can't take this anymore, Carl!" my mom screams at my dad. She storms out of the room in tears.

Dad follows her, trying to calm her down, and I'm left alone with Grandma.

There's no electricity in the family room yet. The only light comes from the hallway and from the bright, full moon. I watch Grandma staring out of the picture window, as if she can see something in the dark, as if she can see the river that the window overlooks. All I can see is darkness.

sanitarium: a hospital for the treatment of people who are very ill

drywall: thin, flat sheets of wallboard, often used in place of plaster

There are tears in her eyes. Even though she is standing right next to me, she seems so far away. So alone.

"Grandma," I ask. "Do you love me?"

"I wish it would stop raining," she says, looking up at the clear, starlit sky. "All this rain, it can't be good for the soil."

"Could you just give me a hug, Grandma—just one hug, like you used to?"

Then, for a moment, I get the feeling that we have had this conversation before. But the feeling is gone in an instant.

For my thirteenth birthday we have a small party with just a few friends. Dad tries to get us to wear stupid party hats, but no one wants to. Grandma sits alone on a folding chair out in the unfinished family room, staring at the unpainted wall across the room, occasionally chuckling to herself.

We all eat ice cream and everyone sings "Happy Birthday"—everyone except Grandma. A few minutes later I notice that one of my dumb friends has put a party hat on her. I go into the family room and take the hat off.

"Have you ever seen the river like this?" Grandma says to the dry, sunny day. "All swollen from the rain? It has to stop raining soon."

For a strange moment, as I hold that party hat in my hands, I get the feeling again that I've done this before . . . but I know I haven't.

Party hat, I think. *Wasn't Grandma talking about a party hat a few weeks ago?* But everyone calls me back into the living room to open my presents, so I don't think about it anymore.

PREDICT

Why do you think Leslie gets the feeling that she has had this conversation before?

For my birthday I get a puppy.

The next night it begins to rain. Troubled by the thunder and lightning, I stay up late and watch TV with Mom and Dad in the living room. Magoo, my new dog, sits by the side of the green velvet chair. On TV a rock band plays wild music. Mom and Dad think it's awful, but I kind of like it. And then I notice . . .

The guys in the band all have pink hair . . . and at the end of the song they smash their guitars.

A chill runs through my body. I look for Grandma, but she is not in the room.

"What's wrong, Leslie?" asks Mom. "Are you all right?"

"I don't know," I say. "I just feel . . . funny."

Bam! The thunder crashes at the same moment the lightning hits, and the house is plunged into darkness.

Dad is up immediately. "I'll get the candles," he says. He feels around for the walls in the dark, like a blind man.

A few minutes later, with a candle in my hand, I search the house for Grandma. I find her in the garage, looking through boxes of old photos.

"Can't leave these behind," she says. "Have to take them with me."

"Grandma," I ask, just beginning to understand. "Where are you? What do you see?"

"Barry, you and your family should never have come to visit with the weather like this," says Grandma. "You should have told them not to come, Carl. You can do what you like, but I'm not taking the chance. I'm getting my stuff, and I'm getting out. Before it's too late."

I can tell she's talking to my Dad and Uncle Barry—but Uncle Barry and his family live a thousand miles away in Michigan, and they haven't visited us for years. Yet Grandma's talking to them like they're in the room.

And suddenly I realize what's wrong with Grandma.

"Grandma," I say. "I know what's happening. I understand now."

PREDICT

What does Leslie know?

What is wrong

with Grandma?

"Leslie, your imagination is running away with you," says Dad. He's sitting in the family room holding a candle. The lights have been out for an hour now. I stand at the entrance to the family room. Mom and Dad sit in a corner. They're talking about putting Grandma into a home or a sanitarium.

"No!" I insist. "It's true. Grandma is living in the future. She's not crazy."

"Get some rest," says Mom. "You'll feel better in the morning."

"No, I won't!" I shout. "Don't you get it?" I stand in the doorway of the family room. "This doorway used to be a wall—this used to be the wall that Grandma would talk to—but she wasn't talking to the wall, she was talking to us inside the family room. Only the family room hadn't been built yet! And when she was pretending to eat ice cream in the middle of the night, she was seeing my birthday party a month later. And when she watches the TV when it's off, she's seeing TV shows that won't be on for a whole month. I even caught her petting the dog *before* we had the dog. And remember when she stood in the family room screaming into the corner about your wanting to send her

What other details prove that Grandma is living in the future?

thrashing: moving about wildly

away? Well, she was screaming into the corner you're sitting in right now! She *saw* the conversation you're having right now, and it really upset her!"

I clench my fists, trying to get Mom and Dad to understand. "Don't you see? Grandma's body might be stuck in the present, but her mind is living a month in the future." I pointed to the grandfather clock down the hall. "It's like how that clock always runs too fast. At first it's just a couple of minutes off, but if we don't reset it, it could run hours—even days—ahead of where it's supposed to be! Grandma's like that clock, only she can't be fixed!"

Lightning flashes in the sky, and Mom stands up. "I think this storm is giving us all the creeps. I'll feel better when it's over tomorrow."

"No," I say. "According to Grandma, the storm goes on for weeks and weeks."

That's when we hear Grandma screaming.

We run into the bedroom to find Grandma <u>thrashing</u> around the room, bumping into things. She clutches the bedpost, holding on for dear life, as if something is trying to drag her away. Mom and Dad try to grab her but she doesn't see them; she just keeps on thrashing and clinging to the bedpost, like a flag twisting in the wind.

"Barry!" she screams. "Hold on! Carl! Don't let go!"

Dad grabs her and holds her, but she is stronger than any of us realize. There is sheer terror in her eyes, and I try to imagine what she sees. "Holly's gone, Carl—Holly, Barry, Alice, the twins, they're all gone—there's nothing you can do! Now you have to save yourself! No, don't let go! No!"

She screams one last bloodcurdling scream that ends with a gurgling, as if she were drowning. Then, silence.

And that's when I know Grandma is gone.

She's still breathing, her heart is still beating, but she is limp and her eyes are unseeing. Her mind has died, but her body doesn't know it yet. It will in several weeks, I think.

Suddenly, the only sound I hear is the falling rain and the rushing of the river a hundred yards beyond our backyard.

That was almost a month ago. Now I stand in my room, shoving everything I care about into my backpack, making sure I leave room for Magoo. I don't let Mom and Dad know what I'm doing. I can't let them know, or they would stop me.

In the family room, which has been painted, carpeted, and furnished, Mom makes up the sofa bed. "Uncle Barry and Aunt Alice won't mind sleeping on this," says Mom, patting the bed. "The twins can sleep in your room," she tells me. "You can stay with us. It's only a week—I don't want to hear you complaining."

But I'm not complaining.

"Isn't it wonderful that they're coming all the way from Michigan to spend some time with us?" says Mom. "After all these years?"

"I just wish we had better weather. I've never seen it rain this much," says Dad, coming into the room. "It can't be good for the soil."

That night, I give Mom and Dad a powerful hug and kiss good night, holding them like I'll never let them go. Then,

PREDICT

What will happen to Leslie? What will happen to her family? What details in the text make you think as you do?

after everyone's asleep, I go into Grandma's room. She lies in bed, as she has for a whole month now. Not moving, barely even breathing.

I give her a hug also, and then I climb out of the window into the rain.

It is raining so hard that in moments I am drenched from head to toe. I am cold and uncomfortable, but I'll be all right.

Tonight I will run away. I don't know where I will go; all I know is that I have to leave. Even now, I can hear the river churning in its bed, roaring with a powerful current ready to spill over its banks.

Tomorrow, after Uncle Barry's family arrives, there will be a disaster. It will be all over the news. There will be special reports about how the river overflowed and flooded the whole valley. The reports will tell how dozens of homes were washed away, and how hundreds of people were killed.

I can't change any of that, because Grandma already saw it. She saw my mom, my dad, my uncle, my aunt, and my cousins taken away by the flood. Then, finally, the waters took her as well. She saw it more than a month ago.

But on that day when we watched her in her bedroom, holding on to her bedpost, torn by waters that we could not see, there was one name she didn't mention. She didn't mention me. And if I wasn't there, then at least one member of my family will have a future.

So tonight I take the high road out of town. And tomorrow I won't watch the news.

Why does Leslie think she will be saved from the flood?

SCREAMING AT THE WALL

▼ Learning from the Story

"Screaming at the Wall" has a complicated plot. Part of the story, the grandmother's part, takes place a month before everything else. Working with several other students, identify the steps in the plot on a long, thin strip of paper marked off in squares. Write each event in the story in a different square.

Cut out the squares that include Grandma's forecasts or foreshadowing of the future. Place these where they really belong in the story. How do her predictions compare with what actually happened?

▼ Putting It into Practice

You've plotted the events in your mystery. You've probably written your draft in chronological order. Now you can experiment with other ways to organize the plot. For example, you might start halfway through your mystery—with an action-packed scene that will grab your reader's attention. You can always flash back to the beginning later. You might start with a dream that foreshadows events that will happen much later. If you type your story into a computer, it's easy to rearrange and print out several versions of your mystery until you find just the right one.

Night Rider

It was a dark and stormy night. . . . What do you expect when a story begins like this?

Rachel Warren flinched as a jagged bolt of lightning split the sky. She looked out the basement window, watching the driving rain drum against the window. A few seconds later a clap of thunder rattled the panes. "Just my luck," she moaned. "The first night I'm allowed to drive the car, and a monster thunderstorm blows in out of nowhere."

"Are you going to play or not?" Debbie Walters asked, ignoring Rachel's complaint. She was sitting cross-legged over a Monopoly game in progress. "It's your turn," she said, handing the dice to her friend.

But before Rachel could reply, the basement glowed as another lightning bolt snapped outside, then the house seemed to shudder as a deafening clap of thunder exploded seconds later.

"Wow! That almost felt like it was *inside*!" Suzanne Murray exclaimed, as she came downstairs from the kitchen, balancing a bowl of popcorn and three sodas. "I'm glad we're staying in the rest of the night."

"I can't believe you're still hungry," Debbie moaned, rubbing her stomach. "I can't even finish this," she added, pointing to the goopy remains of a hot fudge sundae. A few hours earlier, on her way over to Suzanne's, Rachel had stopped at Scoops Ice Cream Shoppe to surprise her friends with a treat.

Sighing, Rachel turned from the window and plunked down at her place next to her friends. Then she picked up the dice and rolled them <u>absentmindedly</u>. She hardly reacted when she landed in jail, which was unusual. Her Friday night Monopoly games with her friends had become a regular <u>rivalry</u> over the past few months. Most nights, the three girls played until long after midnight, then slept on the couches and chairs in Suzanne's family room.

Tonight, though, was the first time Rachel had been allowed to take her mother's car, and she was too <u>preoccupied</u> to enjoy the game. She couldn't stop thinking about driving home in the storm. She'd only gotten her driver's license the day before, and her mother had allowed her to take the car across town to the Murrays' house only if Rachel promised to be home by midnight. Now, instead of staying overnight at Suzanne's, Rachel had to keep an eye on her watch and drive home in the unexpected storm. She just couldn't call home and say she was scared. If she did, her folks would *never* let her take the car again. Besides, she was supposed to be able to drive in all weather conditions. Now was the time to prove it.

"Earth calling Rachel," Debbie said in a teasing voice. "Come on, it's your turn again."

absentmindedly: without paying attention to what is going on

rivalry: competition

preoccupied: lost in thought about something else

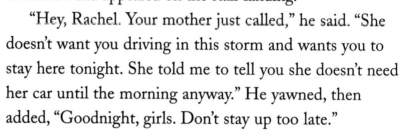

"Huh?" Rachel grunted, not noticing she'd daydreamed through another round. "Oh, sorry," she said, picking up the dice. As she did, she glanced at her watch. It was 11:25. She'd better go soon. She was about to say that this would be her last throw when Suzanne's dad appeared on the stair landing.

"Hey, Rachel. Your mother just called," he said. "She doesn't want you driving in this storm and wants you to stay here tonight. She told me to tell you she doesn't need her car until the morning anyway." He yawned, then added, "Goodnight, girls. Don't stay up too late."

Why do you think the author included this phone call? What does it add to the plot?

"Well, isn't that great," Rachel said sarcastically. "My parents think I'm not capable of driving in a little rain."

"Look outside," Debbie said. "It's a *lot* of rain."

"Well, I don't care," Rachel said stubbornly. "I'm driving home to prove I can drive under any conditions."

"You're crazy, Rachel," Suzanne protested. "It's dangerous out there."

"Suzanne is right," Debbie said. "You don't have to prove anything."

"And you guys don't need to say anything to Suzanne's parents when I leave, right?" Rachel said, raising an eyebrow. "Come on," she added, seeing her friends hesitate. "I'm doing this for all of us. If we don't prove we're good enough drivers to drive in a freak storm, we'll never get to use our parents' cars."

Slowly, Debbie and Suzanne nodded their agreement. Then Rachel grabbed her car keys and slipped out of the house into the pouring rain.

As she drove along, Rachel had the windshield wipers on full blast, but she was still having trouble seeing through the blinding downpour. She was beginning to think that she wasn't going to prove anything to her parents except that she was an idiot for not listening to them. Suddenly a news bulletin broke into the country-and-western song she was listening to on the radio.

"Thirty minutes ago, we reported that three inmates from the Whiting Institute for the Criminally Insane escaped," the announcer said. "We are now pleased to report that two of the inmates have been captured. However, one is still at large. That man is said to be Marty Bronson, otherwise known as 'The Panther.' Bronson got this nickname because of a large black-panther tattoo on his right arm. Officials at the Whiting Institute claim that Bronson is very dangerous and—"

But Rachel's mind tuned out the rest of what the announcer was saying. Terrified, all she could think about was how Bronson was probably somewhere nearby. After all, the Whiting Institute was right in between her house and Suzanne's!

"I can't believe this. Not only do I have to drive home in this mess, I've got to keep an eye out for some wacko with a tattoo!" Rachel grumbled, as she fumbled with the radio to find another station. She didn't know if she wanted to find a good song or a news channel so she could keep on top of whether or not Bronson had been located.

PREDICT

Will Rachel get home safely? What details make you think as you do?

"Well, just stay cool, Rachel," she said to herself, trying to stay calm. "You'll be home in no time," she added, glancing at the speedometer to make certain she didn't go over the speed limit in her rush to get there.

Suddenly, as she scanned the dashboard, her heart sank. The gas gauge was on empty. "That was stupid," Rachel scolded herself. "Mom warned me to get gas before I went to Suzanne's." She looked at her watch and frowned. She was going to be home past midnight, but she had to stop for gas.

At the entrance ramp to River Drive, Rachel pulled into a gas station. The rain was a thick mist now, and Rachel shivered in the moist air as she got out to pump the gas.

Yanking her baseball cap low over her frizzy brown hair, she hurried over to the clerk and shoved a ten-dollar bill through the slit in the glass. *That ought to buy enough gas for Mom to get around for the next few days*, she thought as the clerk, a large bearded man, grabbed the money.

Rachel's eyes widened. Peeking out from under the rolled-up sleeve of the man's shirt was part of a tattoo.

Is that a panther? she wondered, unaware that she was staring at the dark shape.

"What are you looking at, kid?" the man growled, pulling up his sleeve to reveal a horse with wings. "Haven't you ever seen a tattoo before?"

Her face burning with embarrassment, Rachel mumbled some kind of apology and rushed off to pump the gas. Then she jumped into her car and sped off, her hands trembling on the wheel.

How does the description of the gas station attendant build suspense? List some other details that add suspense to the story.

A half-mile down the road she came to River Drive, a four-lane highway that bypassed downtown. Slightly increasing her speed as she entered the highway, Rachel was hoping she could make up for lost time when suddenly she noticed painfully bright headlights right behind her, bouncing off her rearview mirror and nearly blinding her.

Who is that jerk? Rachel thought. *Doesn't he know I can't see with his high beams shining in my eyes?*

"I'm being followed," she said

softly, shivering not from the dampness

but from an ever-increasing tremor of fear

running through her entire body.

As far as Rachel could make out, the lights seemed to be coming from a large pickup truck. She slowed down to let it pass, but it slowed, too . . . and pulled even closer. Her heart racing, Rachel increased her speed, but the pickup roared right up behind her.

"I'm being followed," she said softly, shivering not from the dampness but from an ever-increasing <u>tremor</u> of fear running through her entire body. The truck was now practically glued to her rear bumper.

Fighting off waves of panic, Rachel turned down her rearview mirror, so the lights no longer hurt her eyes.

tremor: a trembling or shaking

But the truck was still so close to her that its headlight beams filled her whole car with an unearthly glow.

What does he want? Rachel thought. *Why doesn't he leave me alone?*

Her hands clutching the steering wheel so hard they hurt, Rachel saw the sign for her exit, only a mile away. From there the roads to her house were dark and winding. She had to make a quick decision. Should she turn off or stay on the highway and hope to pass a police car?

Suddenly a relieving thought hit her. "What a jerk I am!" she said out loud, trying to sound brave. "That truck isn't following me." She put on her right turn signal and slowed for the exit. "It's probably just some kids clowning around trying to scare me." Rachel laughed nervously. But when she cruised down the ramp, the truck followed. It kept its beams on high, following so close that it almost seemed to be in the car. "Okay," Rachel murmured. "So they're *really* trying to scare me."

Now winding along dark two-lane roads, Rachel frantically tried to figure out what to do. She passed houses and saw lights in a few of the windows, and thought about how inside those homes people were talking or reading or getting ready for bed. They had absolutely no idea that Rachel Warren was being followed by someone who might actually be a <u>maniac</u> known as The Panther!

Pressing on the gas pedal, Rachel picked up speed. She *had* to get home. If she could just get there, she knew she'd be safe.

What should Rachel do? What would you do if you were being followed?

maniac: an insane person

And still the bright lights filled the car.

Finally, Rachel pulled onto her street. She floored the pedal and flew into the driveway, her tires screeching to a stop just before she plowed through the closed garage door. The truck pulled right in behind her, the rumble of its powerful engine shattering the midnight stillness.

Rachel jammed the car in Park and threw open the door. "Leave me alone!" she screamed, running toward the front steps. "Mom! Dad! Help!"

Behind her she heard the truck door slam. Footsteps pounded in her direction. *I'll never make it!* her mind screamed. Then she felt her body go limp. She was falling but could not stop herself. And then everything went black.

Rachel heard a voice coming from above her. "Are you all right, young lady?" someone asked.

Opening her eyes, Rachel realized she was lying face up on the wet sidewalk. Then she saw the bright beam of a flashlight shining on her sweatshirt.

"Everything's okay," a deep voice was <u>reassuring</u> her. "Don't worry."

Rachel sat up and tried to speak. "I—I think I'm okay," she whispered. "I must have fainted. A man was behind me. He—he was going to kill me!"

"No, no," the voice said. "*I* was the man who was following you."

Rachel felt a wave of panic. She squinted past the flashlight beam and saw a stocky man in a blue windbreaker and jeans.

Stop reading. Based on the clues you have read, who do you think was following Rachel?

reassuring: restoring someone's confidence

"You?" she asked, her voice squeaking in fright.

"That's right," the man said gently, then pointed a flashlight beam toward the car. "The guy who was after you is over there. I knocked him out with a tire iron."

Rachel followed the man's flashlight beam toward her car. An icicle of fear passed through her as she saw a large man lying near the front bumper, his hands tied tightly with a belt. She looked from there back to the man holding the light with a horrified look on her face.

"Did you notice any, like, marks on his arm or anything?" she said hoarsely.

"You mean like a tattoo?" the man said. "Yeah, I did, now that you mention it. It looks like some kind of big cat—maybe a panther." He paused as lights came on upstairs. "Is anyone home?" he asked.

"Yeah," Rachel answered, still confused about what had taken place. She tried to stand up, but she felt as shaky as a newborn colt. The man helped her to the front steps and sat beside her. "Thank you," she said. "You saved my life— but can you tell me what happened?"

"Sure," the man said with a warm smile. "I was driving home from work in the right lane on the highway when you came on and cut me off. Anyway, because my truck rides high off the ground, my lights were shining right into your car, and I saw that guy hiding in your backseat. That's when I put on my high beams and <u>tailgated</u> you so he couldn't make a move."

tailgated: drove dangerously close behind another car

Rachel felt dizzy again. She jumped nervously as the porch lights flicked on. Hearing the front door swing open, she tried to stand up to go inside. The man gently took her elbow and helped her up the steps to the doorway.

PREDICT

Is this man telling the truth? The story isn't over yet. What do you think will happen next? Why?

"Rachel?" her father said sleepily. "What's going on? We thought you were staying over at your friend's house."

"Everything's fine now," Rachel said, her voice trembling, "thanks to this nice man. He saved my life."

"What?" her father said, his eyes widening. He quickly opened the door to help Rachel inside. "I think I'd better call the police."

Rachel nodded. "That's a good idea," she said. Then she turned toward the man. "Thank you again, sir. Would you like a drink of water or something?"

"Thanks," he said, removing his torn windbreaker. "But I'd better leave this outside. It's wet and dirty."

Rachel's father smiled gratefully at the man. "I'm not sure what you did, sir," he said, extending his hand. "But thank you."

As the two men shook hands, Rachel stared at the stranger's bare arms jutting out from his white T-shirt and nearly fainted as she heard her father saying, "Gee, that's quite a tattoo you have there. Is that a panther?"

▼ Learning from the Story

The author of "Night Rider" does a great job of building suspense. As you read, you can almost feel how terrified Rachel must have been. Working with several other students, list all the ways the author created suspense. Keep in mind that light, sounds, and even the weather can add to the suspense. Then create a line graph that charts how the level of tension changes from one part of the story to another.

▼ Putting It into Practice

Your story will be presented as a play or a movie. So you can use music, lighting, and sound effects, as well as action, to help you build suspense. Look back over your story. When should you start bringing in some tension-packed music? Where should the lights dim—or go out? When can you add startling sound effects to shatter your viewers' nerves? Try to add these elements gradually, to create a feeling of suspense slowly.

The Quarterback's REVENGE

It happened twenty years ago, but the people in Altamonte Heights still remembered. Oh, they didn't talk about it much. Mostly, they wanted to forget. It was a cold, sunny Saturday in November. The team was down by a field goal. With thirty-four seconds on the clock, the Altamonte Crusaders were on their own forty-yard line. If anybody could throw a bomb, it was their quarterback, Alex Koslowski. With no time left, he took the snap and faded back, back . . .

The ball spiraled high. The hundreds of fans in the stadium held their breaths. Dudley leaped into the air. He caught the ball as if it was only another after-school scrimmage, not the biggest game of the year—the state playoffs. When his right foot touched down in the end zone, the fans erupted!

Suddenly, a hush replaced the roar. Koslowski was down. Ten minutes later, an ambulance crew rolled the quarterback off the field. He never regained consciousness.

After the accident, the school seriously considered for a time dropping football from its athletic program. It didn't, but the heart had gone out of the game for a lot of local

It takes a lot of hard work and sacrifice to become a football hero—

MORE THAN YOU'D EVER IMAGINE!

scrimmage: practice play between squads of a football team

people. Especially for Coach Andrew Tyler, who quit his teaching job and never coached another game.

That was twenty years ago, and time does heal. Altamonte had a new, young coach and, more important, a talented quarterback—Herbie Snyder. Herbie had moved to Altamonte Heights from Michigan earlier that year and was burning up the field with his powerful arm. For the Altamonte fans, the game was fun and exciting again. Herbie Snyder took the Crusaders all the way to the state playoffs.

"I can't tell you how important this game is for me," Coach John Tyler told his players in the locker room, four days before they would play Mill Springs for the state title. "I want to win this game for my dad. Some of you may not know it, but he coached at this school twenty years ago when—" Coach Tyler hesitated. *Why bring up bad memories?* "The point is, men," he continued, "this is more than just a game. The door right now is open for every one of you."

"What door is that, Coach?" Herbie asked, grinning. He was enjoying his hero's <u>status</u>.

"The door to a lot of colleges and universities," said Coach. "You've gone the distance, boys. After Saturday, some of you just may walk away with scholarships."

"Do you think the <u>scouts</u> for Notre Dame are going to be there, Coach?" Herbie asked. "I don't want to play for anybody but Notre Dame."

The others laughed. Coach Tyler allowed himself to crack a smile, too. "Don't get cocky on me, Snyder." Then his smile faded. "I don't want anything to go wrong on Saturday."

status: position or rank

scouts: people sent by sports teams to find talented new players

Herbie laughed. "Hey, what could go wrong?"

Later, in the locker room as Herbie was getting dressed, Todd, the second-string quarterback, slapped Herbie playfully on the shoulder. "You know what coach was getting at, don't you?"

"Sure. We all may be fighting for the Irish next year."

"Not that. The part about his dad."

Herbie shrugged.

"I forgot," Todd said, "you're not from around here. So you don't know about the quarterback <u>jinx</u>."

Herbie slammed his locker door closed. "Todd, my man, I don't believe in <u>superstitions</u>, so quit goofing on me."

"I'm not making it up. It happened twenty years ago, the last time Altamonte was in the state playoffs. It was an accident and all, but it was pretty scary."

Herbie glanced at the clock. Karen would be waiting for him outside, but Todd had him hooked. "Okay, so tell. What happened that was *sooo* scary?"

"Well, Coach's dad was calling the shots then. The quarterback was this kid named Alex Koslowski. In the final seconds, Koslowski took a really bad hit."

Herbie felt a shiver slide up his spine. "So?" He tried to sound cool.

"So, the guy didn't make it."

"You mean—?"

Todd nodded grimly. "My dad was playing on the team. He and Alex were best friends. They were both big Miami fans."

"You mean the Hurricanes?"

jinx: something that brings on bad luck

superstitions: beliefs or practices resulting from trust in magic or chance

Why did the author have Todd tell Herbie this story?

Todd nodded. "Seems Alex had even heard from a Miami scout. He wanted to play for them, only he never got the chance."

Herbie knew that every ballplayer got scared sometimes. The best learned how to control their fears, Coach Tyler had told him. Herbie shook his head, clearing away the worry that had begun to cloud his mind. He picked up his gym bag. "That's a sad story, Todd, but it's not going to happen to me. This is my game, not Alex Koslowski's."

"Yeah," Todd said, brightening a little. "The door's open for you, right?"

"Wide open, Todd," Herbie said confidently. "Wide open."

The next night after practice, Herbie found a folded piece of paper taped to the inside of his locker door. "Oooo," Tony said, walking past, "another love note from Karen?"

Herbie laughed as he unfolded the note. He stared at it a moment, then turned to Todd. "Is this your idea of a joke?" Todd took the paper and read, *My game—not yours.* "What do you think it means?"

"Why don't you tell me?"

"What—you think I wrote this?" Todd said, defensively.

"No one else was in the locker room last night when we were talking," Herbie fired back. "No one else heard me say that."

Todd straightened. "Look, I didn't write that note. Why would I?"

Herbie stared hard at Todd. He had no idea why Todd would try to psych him out before the biggest game of their lives, unless Todd was tired of playing second string. Herbie crumpled the note in his fist and walked away.

On Wednesday, Herbie's football jersey was missing. "It was here before we went on the field," he said, eyeing Todd suspiciously.

"This is too weird," Todd said.

"It's not weird," Herbie said angrily. "You're messing with my stuff, and if you don't cut it out, I'm gonna tell Coach you're <u>sabotaging</u> the game."

The other guys in the locker room stopped talking and turned to look at Herbie and Todd. The two quarterbacks were glaring at each other. "C'mon, you two. Knock it off," Tony said. "Save it for the game on Saturday."

Todd backed away. "You're losing it, man," he said, shaking his head.

That night with Karen, Herbie admitted he was nervous. "I'm not scared," he was quick to point out. "Just, you know, nervous."

"Why wouldn't you be?" Karen said. "There's a lot of pressure on you."

"That's right, there is." Herbie sighed. They were standing outside Karen's house, but Herbie had asked her to stay with him a few minutes longer. Karen always knew how to make him feel better about things. She reached for his left hand and turned it palm up.

"Let's see," she teased, tracing a fingertip over his smooth palm. "Oh, yes. I can see it very clearly. You are definitely going to win the game and get a scholarship to—"

PREDICT

Who do you think is leaving Herbie notes and taking his jersey?

sabotaging: damaging; destroying

He grinned. "To where?"

"—the community college right here in Altamonte Heights!"

He snatched his hand away. "No way."

She laughed. "Just kidding. Look, I've got an algebra test tomorrow. Are you okay now?"

He nodded. "Yeah, thanks for listening."

"Todd's just jealous. If anything happened to you, he'd get to play in the big game."

"Todd wouldn't <u>jeopardize</u> the game just so he could play," Herbie said. But the truth was, Herbie wasn't so sure about that.

That night, he tossed in his sleep. After midnight, he bolted out of bed and stood in the middle of his room in the dark, eyes searching for the voice that had whispered in his ear, *"My game . . . my life."* No one was there. He rubbed his eyes. "Just a bad dream," he muttered. "Just a bad dream."

The next afternoon, Coach worked the team hard during practice. Afterward, as the others trotted back to the locker room, he called Herbie aside. "What's up, Herbie? You were distracted out there."

Herbie shrugged. "I'm okay, Coach. I just didn't sleep too well. Thinking about the game and all." He repeated what Karen had told him last night. "There's a lot of pressure on me. A lot of people are counting on me to win this thing."

Coach raised an eyebrow. "Listen up, Herbie. There's no I in *team*. There are ten other players on that field working with you to make this victory happen. Don't you forget that."

jeopardize: to risk; to put in danger

"Yes, sir."

Then the coach <u>relented</u>. He tapped Herbie on the side of the head. "You've got what it takes, kid. You're going to do fine out there on Saturday. Now go home and get some sleep."

Herbie was late getting to the locker room. The others were already dressed and leaving. His right shoulder was sore, and he stayed a long time in the shower, letting the hot water work out the kinks. When he finally turned off the water and stepped out of the shower, the locker room was empty. Standing in front of the steamy mirrors, he began to towel his hair dry. Then he heard it, a soft sound, like leaves rustling.

"My game."

Herbie froze, the towel in his hands.

"My life." It was a low whisper.

"Todd!" Herbie shouted, whirling around. No one was there. Water dripped from the shower heads. Locker doors hung open. But the room was deserted. "Coach?" Herbie called out. No answer. Herbie was alone.

When he looked in the mirror again, he caught his breath. Two faces were staring back at him through the steamy glass—his and another's. The boy was about Herbie's age, but Herbie had never seen him before. *"My life,"* the face said.

"No!" Herbie roared. When he wiped the steam from the mirror with his towel, the face disappeared.

Karen was waiting outside. Everyone else was gone, and Herbie had still not come out. She paced. It was dark, and she was worried. Finally, the gymnasium door opened,

relented: let up; became less harsh

PREDICT

Was your first prediction correct? How would you change your prediction about who's responsible for shaking up Herbie?

and Herbie hurried out, his football jacket unbuttoned. His face was white. What he told her was too incredible.

"Are you sure you didn't imagine it?" she asked.

"I saw him," Herbie repeated. "He had curly brown hair. Kind of long and shaggy against his neck. He was taller than me. I saw him, Karen. I did."

"Okay, okay. I believe you saw. . . " she hesitated. "Someone."

"No, I saw *him*. Koslowski. The quarterback."

"Herbie, listen to me." Karen spoke softly. "Alex Koslowski died twenty years ago."

"All I know is what I saw. And heard."

Karen sighed. "Let me prove it to you. Come with me." "Where?"

"Just come," she insisted.

Karen handed her request to the research librarian. "Can we see this on <u>microfilm</u>?"

The librarian read the date Karen had scribbled on the piece of paper. "Twenty years ago? Yes, we have this in the back room."

A moment later, the librarian returned with the box of microfilm. Karen led Herbie to a large machine at the rear of the building where she threaded the film over the wheels. As the tape whizzed through the machine, **microfilm:** photographs time spun backwards. Days and weeks ticked off in of newspaper and seconds. "Here," Karen said, stopping the machine and magazine pages focusing on the headline of the *Altamonte Heights Courier*. preserved on film "Oh no!" she gasped.

"It's him!" Herbie cried.

The boy with the dark, curly hair was staring at them from the screen. His eyes were dark and determined. But what had startled Karen was the headline on Alex Koslowski's <u>obituary</u>: *His Game, His Life.*

"That's what you heard, isn't it?" she asked, unable to tear her eyes from the screen.

Herbie nodded. He could not speak.

A second picture of Alex showed him in uniform, right arm cocked, ready to throw the ball, left arm extended palm up toward the camera as if blocking a tackle. "Look. He had a scar on his left palm," said Karen.

Herbie flipped the light off on the machine, and the image of Alex Koslowski faded into darkness. "Okay," he said, his voice no longer wavering and frightened. "So Koslowski is dead. Now I know that what I saw tonight really was just my imagination." He shook his head, smiling. "Crazy stuff, huh? Stress and all that. Let's get out of here."

"But you described him just the way he looked—" Karen protested.

Herbie shrugged. "Coincidence. Curly hair, tall—that could describe anybody."

"Those eyes," she said and shuddered. "They were so piercing, as if he really was looking out at us from the machine."

Herbie laughed at her. "No one believes in ghosts, Karen."

Karen said nothing. She rewound the film and returned it to the librarian. They walked home in silence. But before going into her house, Karen looked into Herbie's eyes and begged him not to play on Saturday.

obituary: notice of someone's death in the newspaper

"What? I have to. And I want to. This is the game of my life!"

"Please," she said. "I'm scared."

"Look, Karen, how would it sound if I went to Coach and said, 'I had a dream about this Koslowski dude and I'm not going to play today.' Or better yet, I could tell him his ghost appeared to me in the locker room. Right. Coach would think I was nuts."

"Then just say you're sick."

"Karen, I can always count on you to help me. You took me to the library and showed me the proof: Koslowski is dead."

If you were Herbie, would you play in the game? Why or why not?

Saturday was cold but sunny. Through three quarters, Herbie struggled to get the Crusaders on the scoreboard. He couldn't seem to connect on his long passes, and the other team sacked him eight times. By the fourth quarter, the score was Mill Springs 6, Altamonte Heights 0. Herbie was bruised sore from the beating he had taken. The Crusaders were on their own forty with less than a minute left on the clock. In the huddle, Herbie called the play. "Go long, Tony," he said. "Just get down there."

"I'll be there," said Tony. "Just hit me this time."

The huddle broke. The center snapped the ball. Herbie faded back, back . . .

Then Herbie heard, like a tiny voice inside his helmet. *My game . . .*

A Mill Springs guard broke through the line and dove for Herbie.

My life . . .

Herbie got the ball off. The pigskin spiraled high in the air. Tony leaped, caught it, and touched it down in the end zone. The fans went wild.

But suddenly, their cheers stopped. Herbie Snyder was down and very still. In the stands, Karen screamed. She pushed her way out of the bleachers and rushed down the concrete stadium steps. A security officer stopped her at the gate to the field. "Sorry, miss," he said.

"You don't understand. He's my boyfriend!"

On the field, Herbie opened his eyes. He saw the face of the tall, curly-haired boy leaning over him. "Don't move," Koslowski said. "Everything is going to be all right."

"No," Herbie murmured. Then everything went dark.

"He's a lucky boy," the doctor said later that night. "Only a <u>concussion</u>. We'll keep him in the hospital until tomorrow to make sure, but I'm positive he's going to be as good as new."

Herbie's parents smiled in relief. They squeezed Karen's shoulder. "Can I see him now?" she asked.

Herbie's mother smiled. "Sure. We'll wait out here."

Karen opened the door. Herbie was lying in the hospital bed. He smiled when he saw her. "Oh, Herbie," she cried. "I was *so* scared!" She stood beside his bed.

"I guess I really am a football hero now," he said. "I won the game, didn't I?"

"You sure did." She beamed. "Are you all right?"

"Just a couple of black eyes, that's all." He smiled. "But I feel like I've been asleep for years." He held out his left hand to her. "Come closer, Karen."

PREDICT

Will Herbie be all right?

What do you think will happen to him?

concussion: an injury to the brain, caused by a fall or a blow to the head

As she reached for his hand, she noticed a long white scar across his palm. It hadn't been there yesterday.

"Did you get that—" She stared at Herbie, unable to finish her sentence.

"What?" he said. "Oh, that? I fell off my bike when I was a kid. You know that hill on Pine Street?"

"Pine Street? You mean, right here in Altamonte Heights?"

"Yeah. I cut my hand real bad."

Karen frowned. "But Herbie, I thought you grew up in Michigan."

"Oh," he said. "Yeah. Guess I'm mixed up. Banged on the head and all." He winked.

Karen couldn't remember Herbie's ever winking at her. He said guys looked nerdy when they tried to impress girls by winking at them.

"Why are you staring at me like that?" Herbie asked.

There was something different about him. She wasn't sure what it was. His face was bruised and the skin around his eyes swollen and dark, but it wasn't that. It was the way he was looking at her. "Your eyes," she began.

Then the door opened and Todd, Tony, and a few other guys from the team piled into the room, crowding around Herbie's bed. "Hey, Mr. Quarterback, Mr. State Champion," they laughed. "Didn't Notre Dame send you any flowers?"

Herbie made a face. "Why would I want flowers from Notre Dame? Now maybe a basket of oranges from the Hurricanes, that would be nice."

Karen looked at him quickly. Notre Dame was Herbie's favorite team.

What clues does Karen have that Herbie is not himself?

"You were out cold, man," Todd said. "You had us all scared."

"Yeah," said Herbie seriously. "It's great to be back among the living."

Karen felt as if the breath were being squeezed out of her. She dropped Herbie's hand and stepped back. The scar . . . the scar hadn't been there yesterday. She was sure of it.

Herbie leaned forward and took her wrist. "Where are you going, Karen?"

His eyes . . . they were dark and staring hard at her. They were not Herbie's eyes. Karen smiled weakly. "I thought maybe you'd want to talk to the guys awhile— you know, alone."

But his fingers tightened around her arm. "Don't go, Karen."

"I have to." She tried to pull away from him. "Let me go."

"No," he said. "Stay." He pulled her toward him, his eyes staring deep into hers. With his mouth so close she could feel his cold breath against her ear, he whispered, "What are you afraid of, Karen? No one believes in ghosts."

The Quarterback's REVENGE

▼ Learning from the Story

Alex Koslowski and Herbie Snyder were both talented quarterbacks at Altamonte Heights High School, but that's where the similarity ends. Working with several other students, create a chart that compares Alex and Herbie. Compare and contrast their personalities, physical appearance, backgrounds, and preferences. Add information that might describe each character. If you were going to make a movie of the story, whom would you pick to play the two characters?

▼ Putting It into Practice

In many mysteries, the detective is a well-rounded, complete character and the suspects are flat, cardboard characters with just one identifying trait.

Think about the traits that make the characters in your mystery unique. Then create cardboard cutouts of all your characters. On the back of your detective cutout, list all of his or her identifying character traits. On each of the suspect cutouts, list at least one trait that separates that character from everyone else.

Hide -and- Seek

Nick's father handed him a slip of paper. "Here's the number of the restaurant where we'll be in case of an emergency," he said. "Remember, only call us if it's something really important."

"Everything's going to be fine," Nick assured his father. "I'm twelve years old now. I can baby-sit a nine-year-old for two hours. Go and have fun."

"Vince, you're to obey Nick while we're gone," their mother instructed Nick's younger brother. "Remember, he's in charge."

"You mean, I have to do whatever he says?" Vince asked fearfully.

"Everything within reason," his mother replied.

"What if he tells me to jump off the roof?" asked Vince. "Or eat a goldfish? Or give him all my toys?"

"I wouldn't do that," Nick scoffed, although the idea of having Vince clean his room *had* crossed his mind.

"No, you wouldn't," Nick's mother warned him.

"Let's go, honey," his father said impatiently, opening the front door. "Nick, be sure to double-lock the door after we leave."

Who would have thought that a stupid little kid's game would turn out like this?

"And don't open it for anyone," his mother added.

"I said, we'll be fine!" Nick insisted, motioning his parents out the door.

His parents hesitated another moment, then finally relented and left the house. As soon as the door was shut, Nick tripped the deadbolt lock.

"Did you double-lock the door?" his father called from the other side.

"It's locked!" Nick shouted back, then turned and headed into the living room.

This was Nick D'Angelo's first time baby-sitting for his brother, and he was eager to prove he could handle the responsibility. Many of his friends at school had been staying by themselves for months, and Nick had been feeling frustrated whenever his folks hired someone else to stay with them—especially when that sitter turned out to be a teenager who was only a few years older than he was. For weeks he had been insisting he could stay home alone, and he wanted desperately to be given that chance. Now, here it was. Tonight, Nick D'Angelo was going to prove to the world that he could be a responsible young adult. The fact that his parents were paying him three dollars an hour to do so only sweetened the deal.

"So, what are we gonna do?" Vince asked eagerly.

"Watch television," Nick replied matter-of-factly as he plopped himself down in front of their big-screen TV. "There's a cool movie on cable I've been wanting to see."

"Can we play a game?" Vince asked.

"No," Nick replied, grabbing the remote control off the coffee table.

"But the movie doesn't start for fifteen minutes," Vince whined, pointing to the program guide. "And I want to play a game. When Betty Stevens sits with us, she always plays games."

"Betty Stevens is a nerd," said Nick, referring to the gawky sixteen-year-old who'd been their <u>primary</u> sitter for the past year. "I mean, if she had a life, she'd be out on dates instead of baby-sitting us."

Vince sat in the chair across from Nick and pouted silently for several seconds. Then he glared up at his big brother, wearing a particularly nasty expression.

"If you don't play a game with me, I'll tell Mom you took money from her cookie jar," he threatened.

Nick sat up with a start. For years, their mother had stored loose change and dollar bills in a ceramic cookie jar on their kitchen counter. Lately, Nick had been "borrowing" from the jar to buy trading cards, snacks, and other odd items when his allowance money ran out. He thought no one knew about these activities, least of all Vince. And maybe Vince didn't know. Maybe he was just bluffing. But Nick knew he couldn't afford to take that chance. Although he had every intention of giving the money back—it now added up to about $12.75—he knew that if his mom ever found out what he'd been up to, she'd probably ground him for a month just on <u>principle</u>. He couldn't afford to take that chance.

"Fine!" Nick snapped, throwing the remote onto the couch. "I'll play with you for fifteen minutes. What do you want to play?"

"How about Dragon's Tooth?" Vince asked, referring to a board game he'd gotten for his last birthday.

primary: main; usual

principle: a rule or code of behavior

What makes this conversation sound natural? How would you compare it to an argument you might have with your brother?

"No way," Nick replied. "It's boring."

"You want to set up my road race track?" Vince asked, his eyes dancing with anticipation.

"Takes too long," Nick stated. "I'll miss the movie."

"Then how about hide-and-seek?" Vince proposed.

Nick considered this. They'd used up every decent hiding place in previous games. That meant that any game they might play now would be over in no time.

"Great," Nick agreed. "Hide-and-seek it is."

"I'll count to thirty and you hide," said Vince, turning away and closing his eyes. "One, two, three . . ."

Immediately, Nick ran for the stairs. He bounded up them two at a time, then turned right into the guest bathroom. Treading as lightly as possible, he stepped into the bathtub and arranged the vinyl shower curtain so it hid his body from view.

As hiding places went, this one was pretty lame, but Nick didn't care. He just wanted to end the game as soon as possible. Then Vince would leave him alone.

"Ready or not, here I come!" Nick heard his brother call from downstairs. <u>Instinctively</u>, he held his breath and tried not to move. Although he had no serious hopes of remaining hidden, the competitive part of his nature refused to let Vince win too easily. He was reminded of those times when he had had to abandon one of his video games right in the middle of a round because he'd been called down to dinner. Sure, he wasn't going to lose money or anything by just walking away from it, and he could work his way back to where he was at any time, but still there was something

instinctively: without thinking; naturally

almost, well, criminal, about not playing your very best. In fact, the hardest thing for Nick to do was to *try* to lose.

"I know you're up here!" Vince called tauntingly as he stood just outside the bathroom door. "I heard you come up the stairs!"

Yeah, a real Sherlock Holmes, Nick thought <u>snidely</u>. *You ought to open your own detective agency.*

He heard Vince step into the bathroom. A moment later, the curtains were pulled back and his brother's eyes glared at him.

"This hiding place *stinks*!" Vince protested. "This wasn't any fun! You didn't even *try*!"

"Hey, I'm twelve years old!" Nick countered. "There aren't that many hiding places I can squeeze into!"

"I want to do it again," Vince insisted.

"Fine," Nick agreed. "But this time, you hide and I'll seek. Let's see how good you are!"

"We have to start in the living room," Vince said, heading for the hallway. "And I'll bet I can hide so well you'll *never* find me."

"Yeah, right," Nick scoffed. "I'll bet I can find you in less than two minutes."

"How much you want to bet?" Vince challenged.

"A quarter," Nick replied, like he was the last of the big-time gamblers.

"Make it fifty cents," Vince countered.

"It's a bet," Nick said as they reached the base of the stairs. "You've got thirty seconds to hide. Then I've got two minutes to find you. Go!"

snidely: in a mean way

PREDICT

Who do you think will win this bet? What details from the story make you think as you do?

Immediately, Nick turned around, shut his eyes, and began counting to himself. He heard his brother thunder up the stairs, then heard the groaning of floorboards overhead as the boy searched frantically for the perfect hiding place. Listening closely for any clues, Nick held his breath. A low rumbling sound would indicate that Vince had opened a sliding closet door. The slap of a wooden door closing was a clue he'd climbed into the linen closet. In fact, having played hide-and-seek with Vince for years, he was by this point able to home in on his brother's location from even the <u>subtlest</u> of noises.

"Twenty-nine, thirty!" Nick declared, spinning on his heels and vaulting up the stairs. "I'm coming to get you, Vince! Better have that fifty cents ready!"

Nick's first stop was the bathroom where he himself had hid just minutes before. Although nothing in the sounds Vince had made indicated that he had returned to this room, Nick figured the kid was just sneaky enough to make it *sound* like he'd gone into one of the bedrooms, then quietly double back and hide in the one place he thought Nick wouldn't bother to look. So, of course, Nick *did* bother to look there, but he found the bathtub empty. "Come out, come out, wherever you are!" he called, checking under the vanity, only to find the usual cleaning supplies and spare rolls of toilet paper.

He next examined the linen closet situated directly outside the guest bathroom, but Vince wasn't in there, either. That left only the three bedrooms.

Deciding to do this <u>systematically</u>, Nick started with his own bedroom. He looked in his closet, under his bed,

subtlest: faintest; quietest

systematically: with some plan or system

beneath his desk, and even in his laundry hamper. His brother was nowhere to be found—yet.

A few steps down the hall to the right was Vince's bedroom. Walking gingerly across the minefield created by all the toys that Vince had left strewn about, Nick quickly did a thorough search of the room. Once again, he came up empty.

By the <u>process of elimination</u>, this left only his parents' bedroom and bathroom.

"I know where you are, Vince!" Nick announced gleefully. "And I've still got a full minute left!"

Moving quickly, he pushed back the mirrored door to his father's closet and searched it from top to bottom. He checked behind his father's business suits and felt around in the darkness behind his pants. No Vince.

He then did the same inspection of his mother's closet. When he and Vince were younger, both boys had had some success hiding stretched out in her packed-to-the-gills closet, effectively <u>camouflaged</u> by their mother's dresses. This time, Nick wasn't going to be fooled. He plowed through his mother's clothes like a heat-seeking missile. Still no Vince.

With his allotted two minutes about to run out, Nick quickly looked under his parents' bed, behind the bedroom drapes, and then in their bathroom's shower stall. Flustered, he realized his time was up.

"Very good, Vince!" he called into empty air. "You won our bet, but I'm still going to find you!"

Deciding to retrace his steps, Nick again searched each bedroom and bathroom top to bottom. He looked behind bookshelves and potted plants, even though there was no

process of elimination: gradually ruling out possibilities

camouflaged: disguised

way a boy as big as Vince could have hidden behind them. But Nick was getting uneasy.

About to give up and ask Vince to reveal himself, Nick suddenly flashed on the answer: *Maybe, while I was in one of the bedrooms, Vince sneaked back downstairs and is hiding there!* It was the only answer that made sense. Vince had faked him out, making him waste his time *up*stairs when he was really *down*stairs.

"It's over now!" Nick cried as he thundered down the carpeted staircase. "I can smell you down here!"

Moving with increasing <u>desperation</u>, Nick did a top-to-bottom search of the living room, the dining room, the kitchen, and the downstairs bathroom. As each inspection failed to produce any sign of his brother, Nick's anxiety rose a notch. Something in his gut told him that something was very, very wrong. There was simply no way Vince could have hidden himself *this* well.

"All right, Vince, I give up!" Nick finally cried in defeat. "Where are you?" He waited for Vince's response, but all he heard was a deathly silence. "This isn't funny anymore, Vince!" he called, a frightened squeak in his voice. "Now come out and show yourself or I'm not going to pay off the bet!"

Nick looked at his watch. It was already eight o'clock. His movie was starting, and now he was going to miss the beginning because of his stupid brother.

"I'm going to watch the movie!" he shouted. "If you want to watch it with me, you'd better come out!"

He listened closely for signs of movement, but still heard nothing. Now Nick was really starting to worry.

Where do you think Vince is hiding? What makes you think this?

desperation: a state of hopelessness leading to panic

He imagined his brother squeezing himself into some impossibly tight space and, unable to breathe, dying of <u>suffocation</u>. Boy, would his parents be upset about that!

"Vince, where are you?" Nick cried, running to the front door on the off-chance Vince had decided to hide outside. But the deadbolt lock was still in place, which meant no one had come or gone since his parents left.

His heart pounding wildly, Nick bounded back up the stairs. Stopping on the landing, he cupped his hands around his mouth like a <u>megaphone</u> and shouted, "Vince!"

"Nick!" came a response. It was Vince's voice, but it sounded faint and strangely far away.

"Vince!" Nick shouted with relief. "Where are you?"

"Nick!" the distant voice called again. "Help me!"

Turning his head from side to side, Nick hurried down the hall toward his parents' bedroom, figuring the calls were coming from there.

"Vince, where are you hiding?" Nick demanded. He paused in the bedroom doorway for his brother's reply.

"I'm over here!" came the faint response. Oddly, Vince's voice now seemed to be coming from the other side of the house, back toward his own bedroom.

"Vince, I mean it! Stop fooling around!" Nick scolded, now feeling an uncomfortable combination of fear and anger. "Just tell me where you are, and I'll help you!"

"I'm back here!" he heard his brother cry. "It's dark!"

Now back in his own bedroom, Nick searched frantically. The faintness of Vince's voice indicated that he was either on the far side of the house or trapped behind something—like a wall!

suffocation: lack of enough air to breathe

megaphone: a cone-shaped device that makes a voice sound louder

Terrified by the possibility that Vince had somehow managed to get himself trapped within the home's superstructure, Nick raced over to his bedroom wall and shouted, "Vince, are you back there? Talk to me!"

He pressed his ear to the papered wall, hoping to hear some sound of movement.

"It's dark, Nick! Help me!" came his brother's tearful plea. But it wasn't coming from behind the wall. It seemed to be coming . . . out of thin air!

Immediately, Nick grabbed a chair, ran over to the air vent above his door, climbed up, and shouted, "Vince, are you in the air ducts?"

"No, Nick, I'm back here!" came a reply so distant Nick could barely hear it.

For the next half hour, Nick raced up and down the stairs calling for his brother. But no matter which room he ran to, Vince's cries seemed to come from someplace else. Finally, Vince's voice grew so faint that Nick was unable to hear it at all. Vince D'Angelo had completely disappeared.

Nick's parents returned from dinner an hour later and he told them the whole story in <u>agonizing</u> detail. At first his mother and father believed the boys were playing some kind of prank—after all, nine-year-old kids don't just vanish into thin air—but the horrified look in their elder son's eyes finally convinced them Vince's disappearance was all too real. Together, the three of them again searched the house from top to bottom, but not only did they fail to find any signs of the missing boy,

agonizing: painful; torturous

they didn't even hear his strange, distant cries for help. Vince was truly gone.

"Where could he have gone?" asked Nick as he joined his mother back downstairs after nearly an hour of <u>fruitless</u> searching. "He sounded so far away. Like he'd fallen into another universe or something."

"I'm going to call the police," his mother declared, moving to the phone. "In the meantime, go back and help your father keep looking."

Exhausted both physically and mentally, Nick dragged himself back up to the second floor. He paused on the landing and looked around for his father.

"Dad?" he called. "Mom wants us to keep looking while she calls the police."

Strangely, there was no reply.

"Dad . . . ?" Nick called again, his voice choked with fear.

"Nick! Where are you?" he heard his father call. "I can't find you!"

The voice sounded impossibly far away.

"Mom! It's Dad!" Nick screamed at the top of his lungs. "Something's happened to him!"

Seconds later, his mother came bounding up the stairs. "Where's your father?" she demanded.

"I—I don't know," Nick stammered in terror. "I think it's the same thing that happened to Vince."

Confused, Nick followed his mother as she ran into the master bedroom. "George, where are you?" she screamed, her voice gripped with fear.

"Over here!" came the faint reply. "I can't see you!"

How would you explain a missing brother to your parents?

fruitless: useless; unsuccessful

Nick watched his mother spin around, trying to find the source of the voice. As she did, she stumbled backward toward the bed—and vanished from sight!

"Mom!" Nick screamed, as he began to reach out toward the spot where his mother had been just a moment before. "Where are—"

"Nick! Stay away from the vortex!" his mother called back faintly. "It's somewhere around the bed!"

"Vortex?" Nick called back. "What's that?"

But his mother's answer was too faint to hear.

Shaking, Nick ran to a dictionary and looked up the word. From what he gathered, *vortex* meant something like the center of a whirlpool. That only meant one thing—his family had been sucked into another <u>dimension</u>!

In that instant, Nick's whole future suddenly flashed before him. He saw himself phoning the police to report the <u>inexplicable</u> disappearance of his father, mother, and brother. He saw a room-to-room search failing to produce any signs of the missing people. He imagined himself being shipped off to a foster home—or, worse, to a mental hospital where faceless doctors in white lab coats would work on him day and night to learn the "truth" of what had really happened here this night.

In that same instant, Nick realized he really had no choice. He belonged with his family, wherever they were. And so, his face <u>devoid</u> of emotion, he closed his eyes and fell toward the bed. As he did, only one thought filled his mind: *Wherever I'm going, I hope it's a nice place.*

dimension: a level of existence or consciousness

inexplicable: impossible to explain

devoid: totally without

Hide -and- Seek

▼ Learning from the Story

The author of "Hide-and-Seek" used dialogue to help his readers understand the relationship between the two brothers. Do you think he succeeded? Why or why not?

Working with three other students, read the story as if it were the script for a play. Assign the following parts: Nick, Vince, the father, and the mother. As you read the story, stop if any of the dialogue sounds strange or doesn't sound like something you'd say. Try to reword the dialogue to sound as natural as possible.

▼ Putting It into Practice

All of the characters in your mystery should have a unique way of expressing themselves. One might stutter, another might have an accent, someone else might try to impress people with a lot of four-syllable words.

Look back at your cardboard characters and see which traits can be conveyed through the words they say. Try reading a paragraph from the story or from a newspaper as each of your characters might read it.

A GRAVE MISTAKE

It was hard to find a summer job in a little town like Dover, Virginia, especially for a couple of fourteen-year-olds. So, even though it was sort of creepy, Carrie Wilde and her best friend, Kelly Stowe, were happy to get work at the Dover Memorial Cemetery for American Soldiers. Their job was to transfer the military records of dead soldiers into the cemetery's new computer system.

One morning, as they were working at their computer stations, down the hall from the office of the cemetery's director, Mr. Riley, Carrie stopped and stared at her screen. "How totally weird," she said.

"What?" asked Kelly.

"I've got a soldier here named Private Noel Rennet who died in an accident on April 29th, 1981, at Fort Albany, Virginia."

"So?" Kelly looked puzzled. "What about him?"

"Noel Rennet was never stationed at Fort Albany," Carrie replied flatly.

Kelly's hands froze over her keyboard. "Did you cross-check the records?"

"Yeah, and here comes the weird part—no one by the name of Noel Rennet has ever served in the armed forces! Not in the army, navy, air corps, or marines. So how come I've got a file here saying he's buried in plot C-147—right here at Dover Memorial?"

"That is freaky," said Kelly, running her fingers through her short-cropped <u>auburn</u> hair.

Carrie jumped to her feet. "Come on," she said. "Let's go find the grave. There has to be an explanation for this."

"I knew I shouldn't have taken this weird job," Kelly said, reluctantly following her friend.

It was a short but creepy walk from the records office to plot C-147. As the girls picked their way through rows of <u>moldering</u> tombstones, they chattered nervously, skirting a few freshly dug graves. Soon they found the plot in question. At its head was a plain marble tombstone etched with PVT. NOEL RENNET: 1944–1981 in simple block letters.

"He was only thirty-eight when he died," said Carrie, doing some simple math in her head.

"That's about all it tells us," said Kelly. "Except we know that his body's buried here."

Carrie shook her head. "Not necessarily. The tombstone gives us a name. But maybe there's some other body in that grave."

"Or maybe no body at all!" exclaimed Kelly. She bit her lip. "Maybe we should go tell Mr. Riley."

"No, he's too busy," Carrie said. "Let's get more information before we bother him."

auburn: reddish brown

moldering: decaying; crumbling

"What kind of information?" asked Kelly, falling into step with Carrie as they headed back through the cemetery.

Carrie shrugged. "I don't know. But I do know where to start looking."

Back in the office, the girls went through every paper they could find with Private Noel Rennet's name on it. There was no information about the accident, but they did find papers regarding how his body was transferred from Fort Albany to Dover.

"It says here," said Kelly, scanning the yellowing documents, "that Rennet's body was handled by Graves Registration." She made a face. "What's that?"

"Mr. Riley told me it's a place where dead soldiers are prepared for transport," Carrie explained.

"Anyway," Kelly went on, "it looks like a guy named Enrique Robles was in charge of transporting the body by train from Fort Albany to Dover Memorial. It arrived here on the morning of April thirtieth and was buried that afternoon, without a ceremony."

Carrie wrinkled her forehead, lost in thought. "That body was moved and buried awful quick," she commented. "How come there was no ceremony? And how come there were no <u>mourners</u>? Didn't Private Rennet have any relatives or friends?"

"It is kind of strange," said Kelly. "But the strangest thing of all to me is that this guy isn't even listed in the armed forces; there's no record of the accident he supposedly had."

"Maybe it didn't happen on the base at Fort Albany. Maybe it happened in a nearby town or something." Carrie's face suddenly lit up with an idea. "Hey, if that's

mourners: people at a funeral who come to grieve

the case, it would have been written about in the newspaper!" She quickly sat down at her computer and booted it up. "Let's <u>access</u> library files on newspapers dated April twenty-ninth and thirtieth," she said, her nails clicking as she worked the keyboard. After a few moments, she exclaimed, "Bingo! Here's an April twenty-ninth article about the death of a soldier from Fort Albany."

"Who was the soldier?" asked Kelly. "Rennet—right?"

"No," answered Carrie. "It was a woman named Corporal Claudia Zucker, and she was hit by a car a couple of miles from the base."

"Do they know who was driving?" Kelly asked, looking over Carrie's shoulder.

"They had only one suspect. Someone by the name of Sergeant Leon Tenner, who disappeared from the base right after the accident." Carrie's fingers played over the keyboard as she reaccessed the Fort Albany records, then peered closer at the monitor. "Tenner apparently made a clean getaway. He was never seen or heard from again."

"Let's see what we can find out about the dead woman, Claudia Zucker," Kelly suggested. "Call up her military record."

Carrie did as she was told, and the two girls learned that Corporal Zucker's maiden name was Robles.

"Now we've got something here!" Carrie almost shouted. "Enrique Robles was the man in charge of getting Noel Rennet's body to Dover. Wow, what a freaky mystery!"

"Let's see if Enrique Robles and Claudia Robles Zucker were related," said Kelly.

PREDICT

What is Leon Tenner's connection to Noel Rennet? What makes you think as you do?

access: enter or use

The two girls stared at Carrie's computer as a mile-long list of names scrolled down the monitor.

"There it is!" Kelly yelped, pointing to two names on the list. "They were brother and sister."

"But we still don't know how all this fits together," Carrie said, stroking her chin. "Robles's sister is killed. Meanwhile, he's <u>escorting</u> the body of a soldier who never existed to this cemetery."

"I think it's about time we 'bothered' Mr. Riley," Kelly said.

Three days later there was an odd gathering of people standing around plot C-147. Along with Carrie and Kelly there were Detective John Howe from the Dover Police Department; Jack Riley, the cemetery director; two army officers; a medical examiner from Fort Albany; and Enrique Robles. They all watched as workmen unearthed the coffin, <u>hoisted</u> it from the grave, and carried it into the <u>morgue</u>.

The medical examiner broke the seal on the coffin and, with an officer's help, slowly opened the lid. Carrie and Kelly held on to each other as the corpse—and a few objects—came into view. There, lying next to the corpse, were several empty water bottles, remnants of food wrappers, and canisters of oxygen. An officer lifted out the canisters and examined the gauges. The indicators were all on empty.

"Obviously," said one of the officers, "an attempt was made to smuggle this man out of Fort Albany in this coffin."

"Most likely," added the medical examiner, "the man died of suffocation or a heart attack. Look at the terror on his face."

escorting: going with someone else, for protection or to show respect

hoisted: lifted up with ropes

morgue: place where dead bodies are kept until identified

The eyes—or what was left of them—were open wide, and the mouth was locked open in a final scream or a gasp for a last breath.

"And look at this." The examiner pointed to flecks of dried blood and deep scratches inside the lid of the coffin. "He died trying to scratch his way out. This man—whoever he is—was buried alive."

A hush settled over the room, then Carrie stepped forward. "The man's name is Leon Tenner," she announced. "He was buried in the Dover Memorial Cemetery under the name Noel Rennet, which is Leon Tenner spelled backward."

PREDICT

Why was this man buried alive? Who did it? Why? What clues make you think as you do?

THE EYES—OR WHAT WAS
LEFT OF THEM—WERE OPEN WIDE,
AND THE MOUTH WAS LOCKED OPEN
IN A FINAL SCREAM OR A GASP
FOR A LAST BREATH.

Now Kelly stepped forward and pointed directly at Enrique Robles. "And this is the man who buried him," she said.

Detective Howe turned to the graying but still muscular man. "You've just had quite an accusation leveled at you, Mr. Robles," he said gravely. "Would you care to ex—"

"It was Tenner's idea!" Robles blurted. "He offered me ten thousand dollars if I would help him <u>desert</u> from the army. The plan was to put him in a coffin with enough food, water, and air to last until he got here to Dover, at

desert: leave the military service without permission

which point I was supposed to let him out." Robles looked relieved to be getting this off his chest. "Tenner was desperate. He told me he'd hit a woman with his car . . . and killed her." Robles stopped and looked at his shoes.

"Go on, Mr. Robles," said Detective Howe.

"Well, I—I boarded the train with Leon Tenner inside the coffin," Robles went on, his voice a little shaky. "And when we reached Dover, a telegram was waiting for me. It—it said that my sister Claudia had been killed."

"By a hit-and-run driver," Carrie said softly. "Right?"

"Yes," Robles said, clenching his jaw. "I—I lost my mind when I realized the man I was helping had killed my sister . . . so, instead of letting him out of the coffin, I . . ." But Robles couldn't finish his sentence. Shrugging, he held out his hands to be cuffed.

"He buried his sister's killer alive," Carrie whispered to Kelly. "That's disgusting!"

Kelly nodded. "Yeah. Tenner sure made a grave mistake by leaving his escape in the hands of his victim's brother."

HOW DID THEY EVER BUILD THIS IMMENSE GRAVE?

THE GREAT PYRAMID AT GIZA

IT'S ONE OF THE ALL-TIME GREAT HISTORY MYSTERIES.

The only surviving example of the Seven Wonders of the Ancient World stands like a massive <u>sentry</u> in the desert sands of the Nile Valley—the Great Pyramid at Giza. Now its darkened passages are hauntingly silent, but one can't help but imagine the awesome burial rituals that must have taken place there when the body of the Egyptian <u>pharaoh</u> Cheops was laid to rest.

The Great Pyramid, flanked by two smaller pyramids, was begun some 45 centuries ago. It took about 30 years to build, with a work force numbering in the hundreds of thousands. Built on the Giza Plateau on the right bank of the Nile about 10 miles from the modern city of Cairo, the pyramid covers 13 acres and is taller than a 40-story building.

Its 2.3 million building stones (enough to build a wall 10 feet high and a foot wide around the entire country of France) weighed from 2.5 to 15 tons each. Amazingly, the four corners of the pyramid are almost perfect right angles, and the sides face the four points of the compass almost exactly. The gleaming white limestone stones that once

sentry: a guard

pharaoh: a king in ancient Egypt

covered the finished pyramid were cut so precisely that not even a hair could be slipped between them.

Though many stones clearly came from the surrounding area, some stones were moved from as far away as 600 miles. How could mere humans have dragged such stones across the scorching desert and then placed them with such astonishing accuracy? The workers probably used barges, sledges, levers, rollers, inclined planes, and reed ropes to painstakingly coax the massive stones into position. It was a feat unequaled in its time.

Within the Great Pyramid there is a central chamber that shelters an empty rose-colored granite sarcophagus, which is a large stone coffin. The coffin probably once held the remains of Cheops (also known as Khufu), who ruled Egypt between 2789 and 2767 B.C. But when the tomb was opened in the ninth century, the body was gone. It's likely that it had been plundered by grave robbers.

HOW COULD MERE
HUMANS HAVE DRAGGED SUCH STONES
ACROSS THE SCORCHING DESERT
AND THEN PLACED THEM WITH SUCH
ASTONISHING ACCURACY?

The Egyptians believed that when their rulers died, they would continue to exist in an afterlife. Things that might be needed in the world beyond the grave were buried with the pharaohs. These things included weapons, food, gold, precious jewels, exquisite furnishings, and many other riches, making the pyramids an attractive target for grave robbers.

To prevent it from being plundered, the King's Chamber of Cheops was constructed near the heart of the pyramid, about 140 feet above the desert floor. The gallery adjoining the chamber had slanting floors, above which huge blocks of stone were braced by timbers. When the pharaoh's mummified body was safe inside the chamber, the timbers were removed and the blocks slid into place, sealing the tomb. Unfortunately, it seems this was not enough to save the tomb of Cheops from thieves.

A Grave Mistake

▼ Learning from the Story

"A Grave Mistake" is set in a cemetery. If you were making a video of the story, where would you shoot it? Working with several students, brainstorm possible locations that you might use. Keep in mind that some of the scenes could be shot in places other than a cemetery—as long as they have the right feel and look. Also discuss lighting and props that would add to the mysterious feel of this story.

▼ Putting It into Practice

By now, you probably have a picture in your mind of the setting for your story. But you need to describe that setting to the director of your movie or play. For each scene, write a paragraph describing the setting. You might describe a location, the furniture needed, the type of lighting. Provide details only if they are important to the story. Give your director and set designer room to create, too.

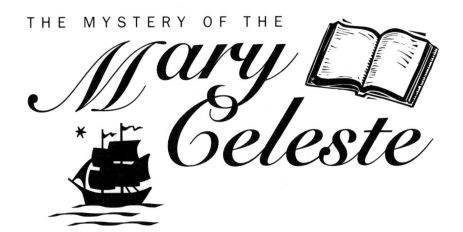

THE MYSTERY OF THE Mary & Celeste

Ricky Steel was surprised to find his mother in their apartment when he came home from school. Linda Steel, an assistant editor at Hadrian House Publishers, always worked long, hard hours and usually didn't get home until seven or later.

"Hi, Mom," said Ricky. "You're home early. What's up?"

Linda Steel, sitting at the kitchen table, looked up into the questioning eyes of her son. "Hi, kiddo," she said, then turned back to the old, weather-beaten book in front of her.

"What are you working on?" asked Ricky, getting a soda from the fridge.

"Something that's driving me nuts," his mother said. "Actually, it's a diary that's supposed to have been found in an attic here in New York City. If it's authentic, it solves one of the weirdest true mysteries of all time."

That got Ricky's attention. "What mystery is that?" he asked, taking a long swallow of soda.

"In December 1872 the captain of a British ship, which was crossing the Atlantic, spotted another ship sailing in a strange, <u>erratic</u> manner," his mother explained. "When the

Sooner or later, you're bound to catch the criminal in a lie. Just hope it happens sooner, instead of later!

erratic: odd; irregular

captain <u>hailed</u> the ship, there was no response, so he sent some of his crew over to investigate. As it turns out, the name of the sailing ship was the *Mary Celeste,* and even though it was sailing across the Atlantic out of New York, there wasn't a single person on board."

"Weird," said Ricky, pulling up a chair. "And you say this is supposed to be a true story?"

. . . "though the ship wasn't sinking, all

the lifeboats were gone. So the question

is, why did all these people abandon

a ship that wasn't even in trouble?"

His mother nodded. "Later, it was found that there had originally been ten people aboard—the captain, Benjamin Briggs; his wife; their baby daughter; and a crew of seven. But the odd thing was, there had been no storms reported in that area of the Atlantic, and most everything seemed to be in good order on the ship. Chests of clothes were dry. There was plenty of food and water. The ship wasn't even leaking. And that's not even the most puzzling part of the mystery."

"What was?" asked Ricky, his eyes growing wide.

"Well," his mother said, obviously pleased that her son was taking such an interest, "though the ship wasn't sinking, all the lifeboats were gone. So the question is, why did all these people abandon a ship that wasn't even in trouble?"

"There must've been something wrong," said Ricky.

hailed: called loudly; shouted

"That's true," his mother said. "The boarding party did find some minor damage. A compass was broken, some of the <u>rigging</u> was broken, and there were gashes in the railing. Over the years, there have been all sorts of theories as to what happened. One is that everyone on board went insane and jumped ship. Another is that a giant squid attacked the ship. Still others claim that pirates, or even aliens, scared everyone." She paused and smiled. "There have been all sorts of theories, but none of them—to this date—have panned out."

Ricky picked up the beaten-up old diary.

"Be careful with that, honey," Ricky's mother said, nervously taking the diary away from him. "It may be worth a lot to my company." She carefully placed the old book back on the kitchen table. "Just a week ago, a woman came into my office claiming that the only survivor from the *Mary Celeste* wrote it. She says she found the diary in her attic, glanced through it, and realized she had stumbled upon the story of what actually happened."

"And what's that?" asked Ricky. History was one of his favorite subjects.

"Supposedly, the diary was written by Ernst Stemmer, one of the crewmen aboard the ship. Stemmer wrote that Captain Briggs caught him stealing, the two got into a fight, and Stemmer killed Briggs with a hatchet. He then grabbed a pistol, killed two other crewmen, and ordered Mrs. Briggs and her baby and the four other crewmen into a lifeboat. He set them adrift without food or water, and they all evidently died at sea.

What is your theory? What do you think happened to the crew of the Mary Celeste?

rigging: lines and chains used aboard a ship to work the sails and support the masts

"For two days, Stemmer sailed alone," Ricky's mother continued. "Afraid of getting caught for murder, he stocked the one remaining lifeboat with provisions and rowed for land, which he reached in three days. Eventually, he made his way back to New York."

"The experts confirm that the paper and ink are both very old. They also say the materials were of the kind that could have been bought around the year 1872 . . ."

Ricky sat back looking satisfied as though he'd just read a good book. "Sounds like it could have happened that way. Don't you think?"

His mother nodded. "Yes, but is the diary itself authentic?" She frowned. "I've been given the job of determining if it's fake or real. The woman who brought it to us at Hadrian House wants twenty thousand dollars. If we publish it and it is authentic, then we have a best seller—and I come out looking great. But if we publish it and it's a fake, then we've not only wasted our money, but Hadrian House becomes the <u>laughingstock</u> of the publishing industry—and I'm probably out of a job."

laughingstock:

something to make

fun of

"Have you had someone test the paper and ink to see how old they are?" asked Ricky.

"The experts confirm that the paper and ink are both very old. They also say the materials are of the kind that could have been bought around the year 1872, when the *Mary Celeste* was found."

"Then it's authentic?" asked Ricky.

"Not necessarily. By using old ink in an old blank diary, and applying moisture and a heat lamp to fade the ink, the whole thing could have been <u>fabricated</u> last week." She sighed. "So I have to decide its authenticity in some other way—by examining every word. So far, I can't find a thing wrong."

"Mind if I take a look at it?" asked Ricky. "I promise to be careful."

"Well, I have been staring at it until I'm cross-eyed. Maybe a break would do me good." She looked at her son sternly. "Remember: This diary—if it's real—is worth a lot."

Ricky took over his mother's seat at the kitchen table and began studying the ancient, yellowing pages of the diary. Now and then he would look up a word in the dictionary or a fact or date in one of the reference books his mother had piled up on the table. In his school notebook, he made notes and copied down entries from the diary.

His mother had fallen asleep on the living room couch long before.

It was ten o'clock when Ricky gently nudged her awake.

"I've got the answer, Mom," he said quietly, sitting down on the couch.

fabricated: invented; made up

She blinked and looked at him sleepily. "Are you sure?" she asked.

Ricky handed her a page from his notebook. On it were written three entries he had copied from the book.

The body of Captain Briggs was lying in the back part of the ship.

I wiped up the blood with paper towels and tossed the hatchet overboard.

The sea was choppy as I started rowing the lifeboat toward the Hawaiian Islands, the nearest body of land, only some five <u>nautical miles</u> away.

Stop reading. What's wrong with each of these statements? How are they proof that the diary is a fake?

"Read the entries a few times," Rick instructed his mother. "Each one proves this diary is a complete fake." He handed her the notebook.

"Do you see what's wrong?" he asked, when she had read them several times.

"Maybe I'm too sleepy," his mother said, yawning as she handed him back the notebook. "Why don't you just tell me what you're getting at, kiddo?"

"In the first entry," Ricky said, eager to explain his theory, "whoever wrote this mentioned, 'the back part of the ship.' A sailor would say 'the stern.'"

His mother smiled. "But maybe he was just an ignorant sailor."

Ricky frowned. "That's possible, I guess. But now look again at the second entry. In this one the writer mentions paper towels." Ricky paused, waiting for his mother to

nautical mile: a measurement of distance on the water, a nautical mile is roughly 6080 feet

catch on. "Don't you see? Paper towels weren't invented until 1907."

Linda Steel sat bolt upright. "And the *Mary Celeste* incident took place in 1872!"

"Which means," said Ricky, beaming proudly, "that whoever wrote this fake diary created a make-believe murderer who used paper towels thirty-five years before they were invented!"

"And the last one's the clincher," said Linda Steel, wide awake now.

"It sure is," said Ricky. "It mentions heading for the Hawaiian Islands."

His mother broke into a wide grin. "Which isn't possible. The *Mary Celeste* was in the Atlantic Ocean—and the Hawaiian Islands are in the Pacific!"

"So," Ricky concluded, "this whole diary is <u>bogus</u>."

"Ricky, you've saved your mother's life!" Linda Steel said excitedly. "Tomorrow is the big meeting where I give my report on whether Hadrian House should buy the rights to the diary. Everybody's going to be there—from the publisher to the woman who gave us the fake diary. I can't wait to see the expression on her face when I put the facts on the table." She put her arm around Ricky and gave him a big kiss on the cheek. "And I can't wait to tell everybody what a smart son I've got!"

bogus: fake; counterfeit

ANCIENT Maps

Some people claim that when Christopher Columbus sailed on his fateful journey to the Americas in 1492, he carried maps showing the approximate position of the western continents. Although the maps have never been found, it is believed they were based on maps that had been drawn nearly 2,000 years earlier. Is it possible that such knowledge existed then? If so, who gathered the information Columbus's maps were based upon?

In 1513, 21 years after Columbus's journey, a map was drawn by a Turkish naval officer named Piri Ibn Haji Memmed, also known as Piri Re'is. He claimed to have based his work on the maps that had been carried by Columbus. Although not perfect, the map detailed South America's interior and western coast, which had not yet been explored by Europeans. The map also showed the coastline of Antarctica as it would appear without ice. But the continent of Antarctica was not officially sighted until 1820!

Why are these maps so surprising? The continent of Antarctica is almost entirely covered by an ice sheet that is in some places two miles thick. The Piri Re'is and other maps indicate that not only did the ancient map makers know about the frozen continent, but they also seem to have known what the land was like under the ice. Such information would have to have been gathered before the ice sheet was as massive as it is now. But the Antarctic ice sheet has existed since well *before* humans have been mapping the globe.

Like rivers, glaciers move or "flow" downhill along the easiest route, so if ancient riverbeds actually exist under the ice, the glaciers would probably follow them.

The Oronteus Finaeus map, copied in 1532 from a mysterious old map, is even more detailed than the Piri Re'is map. It shows the paths of ancient rivers on Antarctica. Modern <u>glaciers</u> appear to follow those same paths. Like rivers, glaciers move or "flow" downhill along the easiest route, so if ancient riverbeds actually exist under the ice, the glaciers would probably follow them.

The Buache map of 1754 is also quite remarkable. On it, Antarctica is drawn as two islands, one much larger than the other, with a narrow channel between. It wasn't until 1955, during the Geophysical Year expeditions, that the underlying structure of Antarctica began to be revealed, including riverbeds, mountains, and the general shape of

glaciers: large masses of ice that never completely melt, even in summer

the land, which appeared to be made up of two parts. Now, satellite imaging has shown the size and shape of the continent, and that it is indeed made up of two parts.

Who were the ancient map makers? Did visitors actually set foot on the continent of Antarctica many centuries ago at a time before the ice had claimed all the land? If so, were they representatives of an ancient civilization that has since disappeared from the face of the earth?

THE MYSTERY OF THE
Mary & Celeste

▼ Learning from the Story

In "The Mystery of the *Mary Celeste*," someone tried to pass off a fictitious diary as the real thing. However, the author of the phony diary included several historical and geographical mistakes in her manuscript. Working with several other students, create your own bogus manuscript. Write a few new pages for the diary of the *Mary Celeste*'s only survivor. Come up with a different explanation for what happened to the crew—only make sure you get your facts straight!

▼ Putting It into Practice

In your mystery, it's only fair to give your readers clues so they can try to figure out who committed the crime. Sometimes it's easiest to work backwards. After you've written a draft and figured out how the crime was committed, go back and sprinkle clues throughout the story. Remember to distract your readers so the clues aren't obvious.

A Case of

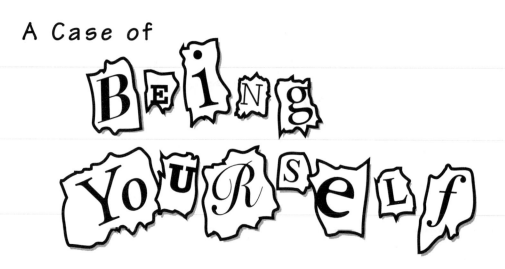

Being Yourself

If you can't be yourself, who can you be?— the victim? the crook? the suspect?

CAST

DANIELLE (DANI) RADEK

DANI'S FRIENDS: ELENA, MATT, JAMAL, KRISTEN

MRS. BARR (a middle-aged woman)

SHERIFF HODGES

MRS. RADEK, DANI'S MOTHER (a police officer)

MR. RADEK, DANI'S FATHER

REPORTER

NARRATOR

SCENE 1

Narrator:	It is lunch time at Selkirk Middle School. Eighth graders Matt, Elena, Jamal, and Kristen are eating at a table in the cafeteria. Dani hurries over to her friends' table. Her eyes are wide with excitement.
Elena:	Hey, what's up, Dani? You look like you're ready to burst.
Dani:	Something big! There's been a kidnapping!

Matt:	*(laughing)* Yeah, right. What TV show do you think we're on?
Dani:	I'm not kidding, Matt. This is for real!
Jamal:	Okay, so talk to us.
Kristen:	Yeah, details, Dani. We want details. *(Dani sits down as the others edge closer.)*
Dani:	On my way here to lunch I saw my mom, Sheriff Hodges, and this woman going into the principal's office. I knew something was up, so I snuck in and listened through the door. The woman was Edna Barr, and it turns out her daughter Cassie was kidnapped.
Elena:	Wow! This *is* big!
Matt:	It sure is! Did you get a chance to talk to your mom, Dani? What does she know?
Dani:	Are you kidding? She'd kill me if she even knew I was <u>eavesdropping</u>. *(Dani looks over her shoulder, then leans closer and whispers.)* But here's what I heard. Mrs. Barr and her daughter just moved into the old Weatherby place on the outskirts of town a couple of days ago. This morning she sent Cassie off to school with her registration papers and a sack lunch, but Cassie never got here.
Jamal:	How do they know it was a kidnapping?
Dani:	Mrs. Barr got a phone call about an hour ago. It was a man with a raspy voice saying he had Cassie and wanted a ransom of $20,000 for her return. He told Mrs. Barr

eavesdropping: listening in on a private conversation

not to contact the cops, but she called anyway. My mom was in the squad room and was the one who took Mrs. Barr's call. No one has a clue as to who would kidnap Cassie—not the school administrators, not the police, not the—

(Dani stops. All five kids turn and watch, as do others in the cafeteria. They see Dani's mom and Sheriff Hodges escorting Mrs. Barr, who is crying and clutching a tissue, from the main building. The three get into a patrol car and drive away.)

Kristen: Oh, that poor woman! I feel so sorry for her.

Matt: I wish we could do something for her. You know, help her find her daughter and put that kidnapper behind bars.

Dani: *(an excited expression coming over her face)* Who's to say we can't?

Jamal: I hear that!

Kristen: The least we can do is try.

Jamal: *(looking from one friend to the other)* Does everyone want in on this?

Dani: *(seeing everyone nod enthusiastically)* Okay, then what we need is some kind of a plan.

Matt: Well, we can't do anything until school's out. But as soon as it is, I say we head for the Weatherby place and talk to Cassie's mom.

Elena: Matt's right. We need to find out as much as we can about the situation before we do anything.

(The bell ending the lunch period rings. The kids get up from the table.)

Dani: Let's meet in front of school at the flagpole. Five minutes after the final bell—and be on time!

Kristen, Jamal: *(together)* Okay.

Elena: Sounds good.

Matt: See you later.

(All hurry off to class.)

What clues do you have so far?

SCENE 2

Narrator: It is after school. Dani, Kristen, Matt, Jamal, and Elena are approaching the old Weatherby place on their bikes. It was once a farm, but the fields are now choked with weeds. The house is old and <u>dilapidated</u>. Out front is a sheriff's car and a battered pickup truck filled with belongings.

(The kids sneak through the weeds, then hide behind shrubs outside an open window. The voices of Sheriff Hodges and Mrs. Barr are coming from inside and can be heard clearly.)

Mrs. Barr: *(her voice tearful and desperate)* What am I going to do, sheriff? All I've got is Cassie. Who would do such a thing? Who would take my baby from me?

Hodges: I've got my people checking the records of any known criminals in the area, Mrs. Barr. And we've got your phone tapped so we can

dilapidated: falling apart

monitor your calls in case the kidnapper tries to contact you again.

Mrs. Barr: *(pleading)* Do you think you'll be able to find Cassie?

All I've got is Cassie. Who would do such a thing? Who would take my baby from me?

Hodges: We'll do our best, ma'am. My deputies are starting a search in a forty-mile <u>radius</u> as we speak.

Mrs. Barr: You've got to find her, sheriff. She's all I have! *(She breaks into loud sobbing.)*

Hodges: *(soothing)* Just try to be positive, Mrs. Barr. Let me handle everything. *(looks at his watch)* Well, I've got to get going. I'd have one of my people come out here and stay with you, but I'm a little short-handed just now and—

Mrs. Barr: *(sniffling)* That's okay. I'll be all right.

Hodges: By the way, the kind of tap we've got on your phone will make a second phone ring in our office at the same time yours rings. If the kidnapper calls again, try to keep him on the line as long as you can so we can trace the call.

radius: a circular area measured by the distance from the center of a circle

Mrs. Barr: *(through tears)* I'll do that, Sheriff.

Narrator:	From where they are hiding, the kids can hear the sound of the sheriff's footsteps. A moment later he drives off in his squad car.
Dani:	*(whispering)* C'mon, you guys.
Elena:	*(to the others)* What's she doing?
Jamal:	Only one way to find out—follow her. *(The others follow Dani onto the front porch. She knocks on the door. Mrs. Barr opens it and is surprised to find the kids there.)*
Mrs. Barr:	Yes?
Dani:	Hello, Mrs. Barr, I'm Dani Radek, and these are my friends Jamal, Matt, Elena, and Kristen. Word got out at our school about what happened to your daughter. *(pausing when she sees Mrs. Barr's startled reaction)* We just came to help.
Kristen:	We can help search the surrounding area.
Matt:	And go door-to-door asking if anyone's seen her.
Jamal:	We can put up flyers around town, too.
Mrs. Barr:	*(seeming confused and bewildered)* Well, I suppose so.
Dani:	Do you have a picture of your daughter we can borrow? You know, to show door-to-door and to put on the flyers.
Matt:	My folks have a photocopier. We can run off a bunch of flyers. All we need is a picture.
Mrs. Barr:	*(turning and heading back into the house)* The sheriff already took one, but I have others.

Narrator:		With Dani in the lead, the kids follow Mrs. Barr into the house. There is almost no furniture, only a beat-up sofa, a couple of lawn chairs, and a table with a phone on it.
Jamal:		*(looking around)* When did you move in, Mrs. Barr?
Mrs. Barr:		Three days ago.
Matt:		*(looking out the window)* I noticed that pickup full of stuff out front. I see you haven't had a chance to unpack yet. Can we give you a hand bringing things in?
Mrs. Barr:		No, that's not necessary. I don't want to put you to any trouble. Besides, I—
Elena:		*(cutting her off)* It's no trouble, Mrs. Barr. Really.
Matt:		We're glad to help in any way we can.
Mrs. Barr:		But—
		(As the other kids go to work, Dani talks to Mrs. Barr.)
Dani:		What was Cassie wearing this morning, Mrs. Barr? Knowing all the details might help us find her.
Mrs. Barr:		Like I told the sheriff, she was wearing a white blouse, a knee-length, pastel-green skirt, and loafers. She has brown hair and . . . *(She stops.)* Here, let me show you a picture.
Narrator:		Dani follows Mrs. Barr into Cassie's bedroom. Unlike the rest of the house, it is completely furnished. A teenage girl's clothes hang in the closet. Above a bed that has

Who's on your list of suspects?

been recently slept in are shelves with <u>knickknacks</u> on them—a jar with dried flowers, an old mug that says "Green Bay Packers," and animal figurines. On a table beside the bed there's a copy of the book *Bambi*, some cassette tapes, and a framed picture of a teenage girl.

Dani: *(picking up the picture)* Is this Cassie?

Mrs. Barr: *(fighting back tears, nods)* People say she looks a lot like me. Do you think so?

Dani: *(gently)* She certainly does. Uh, do you think I could take this photo? *(adding quickly)* Just for a while? *(Mrs. Barr nods and Dani slides the photo out of the frame.)*

Dani: I'll bring this back as soon as we make copies.

Mrs. Barr: You and your friends are so sweet to help me. I really appreciate it. *(Dani pats her on the shoulder as Kristen enters. Idly, Kristen studies the clothing in the closet, then looks at the music cassettes on the table.)*

Kristen: We've almost got your truck unloaded, Mrs. Barr. Is there anything else we can do?

Mrs. Barr: No, thank you, dear. You've all done quite enough already.

Matt: *(Looks in the door. He is carrying a box of sweaters and coats.)* Where would you like me to put this, Mrs. Barr?

Mrs. Barr: *(absentmindedly)* Oh, anywhere is fine.

knickknacks: small decorations, such as figurines

Matt: We put most of the things in the living room, but I guess these clothes should go in the other bedroom, right?

(Matt walks away. Mrs. Barr, seeming very __agitated__ and confused, wanders after him. Kristen and Dani follow her and Matt into the other bedroom. Dust poufs up from the floor as Matt puts the box down. Elena enters with two large shopping bags. She sets them down and puts her hands on her hips.)

Elena: Well, that's about it. Everything's unloaded from the truck.

Mrs. Barr: *(wiping at her tears)* You're so kind. *(She stifles a sob.)* I just hope they find my Cassie and that she gets to be friends with all of you.

Kristen: We do, too, Mrs. Barr.

(Everyone leaves the bedroom.)

Dani: Oh, one last thing, Mrs. Barr. What are Cassie's height and weight?

Mrs. Barr: She's five-foot, six inches tall and weighs about 115 pounds.

(Dani notices a pen and a battered, coffee-stained spiral notebook beside the phone.)

Dani: May I have a sheet of that paper and borrow the pen to write that down, Mrs. Barr?

Mrs. Barr: Certainly. *(She rips a sheet of notebook paper off and hands it and the pen to Dani. The daylight is fading. Dani flips on a light so she can see to write, but the light doesn't work.)*

agitated: disturbed; upset

Mrs. Barr: *(embarrassed)* Uh, I haven't hooked up the electricity yet, but the kitchen gets some afternoon sunlight.

(Dani goes to the kitchen to write down the information she's gathered. Jamal, feeling grungy from carrying boxes, also goes to the kitchen to wash his hands. When he turns the water on, only a rust-brown dribble comes out.)

Mrs. Barr: The, uh, water was just recently turned on. Sorry about that.

Jamal: Doesn't matter. *(He smiles warmly.)* I can wash up when I get home.

Narrator: The kids leave. Mrs. Barr shuts the door behind them. They walk along the road Cassie would have taken to go to school. Matt and Elena are looking for clues. Dani is studying the photo of Cassie. Kristen and Jamal are deep in thought. Suddenly, Dani stops dead in her tracks.

Dani: *(ready to burst with excitement)* I think I saw Cassie at school today!

Elena: Huh?

Jamal: Are you nuts?

Dani: Nope. I'm just a good detective. I'll explain later.

What new pieces of evidence have you uncovered?

SCENE 3

Narrator: Dani is having dinner with her parents. She looks uneasy. She's deciding how to tell her folks she knows about the kidnapping.

Dani: *(picking at her food)* Hey, Mom, guess what? I saw you at school today.

Mrs. Radek: *(puts down her fork and raises her eyebrows in surprise)* Oh, really?

Dani: *(hesitant)* And, uh, I know about the kidnapping.

Mr. Radek: *(looking up)* Kidnapping? What's this about?

Dani: Well, I saw you and Sheriff Hodges going into the principal's office with a crying woman, and I just happened to hear that her name is Mrs. Barr and that her daughter was kidnapped.

Mr. Radek: Dani, this eavesdropping has got to stop. You're always snooping into other people's business.

Dani: *(looks down at her plate)* Sorry. I can't help it if I've got a curious nature.

Mrs. Radek: Have you told anybody else?

Dani: Just Elena, and Matt, and Jamal, and . . . Kristen. And . . . uh . . . we all went out to the old Weatherby place to see Mrs. Barr, and we . . . *(She ends her story mid-sentence.)* Where's Mrs. Barr from, Mom?

Mrs. Radek: From Wisconsin, a little town called Harper. She told us she'd lived there all her life . . . until her husband was killed last year in a boating accident. She moved here to make a fresh start.

Mr. Radek: Poor woman. First she loses her husband and now her daughter.

Mrs. Radek: What's worse is Cassie is her only child. *(sighs)* She sends her off for her first day at school, and just like that the girl vanishes. *(sadly)* Poor thing, she blames herself.

Dani: Why?

Mrs. Radek: She says she offered to drive Cassie to school, or even walk with her. But you know how teenagers are. Cassie said she'd be embarrassed to have her mother take her.

Dani: *(nodding)* Well, I can understand that.

Mrs. Radek: I guess. *(She frowns.)* But what I don't understand is kidnapping the child of a woman who has so little. Mrs. Barr hasn't got a *hundred* dollars in the bank, not to mention twenty *thousand* dollars!

Mr. Radek: How's she going to get that kind of money?

Mrs. Radek: The bank is going to give her a loan.

Mr. Radek: With no credit?

Mrs. Radek: Sheriff Hodges arranged the loan. He'll give it to Mrs. Barr at seven o'clock. Then she's supposed to make the drop by ten tonight at Mason Ridge Park. The kidnapper said to put the money in a plain brown bag and drop it in a trash can by the swings.

Dani: So the kidnapper called again?

(Mrs. Radek shakes her head No as she fishes an envelope from the pocket of her jacket. She takes a piece of notebook paper from the envelope, unfolds it, and puts it on the table. The paper is covered with words cut from a newspaper.)

Mrs. Radek: It has all the instructions for dropping off the money. It tells Mrs. Barr to come on foot, that there will be no more phone calls, and that she has one chance—and only one chance—of getting her daughter back. *(Dani is studying the piece of paper while her father examines the envelope.)*

> It has all the instructions for dropping off the money. It tells Mrs. Barr to come on foot, that there will be no more phone calls, and that she has one chance—and only one chance— of getting her daughter back.

Mr. Radek: How was this delivered?

Mrs. Radek: The envelope was found under the windshield wiper of one of our squad cars.

Mr. Radek: *(to his wife)* I guess you and the other deputies will be staking out the drop site tonight.

Mrs. Radek: *(frowning)* Everybody except me. I wanted to be on the stakeout, but I <u>drew</u> station watch this week. *(shrugs)* Somebody has to be at the station, and that's me. *(looks at her watch, then hastily gets up)* Which reminds me, I'd better get over there pronto.

drew: received an assignment randomly

Mr. Radek: *(getting up and kissing her on the cheek)* You go on, honey. Dani and I will do the dishes.

Mrs. Radek: Thanks. I appreciate it.

(Mrs. Radek hurries from the house and drives off to the station. Dani notices that her mother, in her rush, has left the ransom note on the table. She quickly puts it in her pocket.)

Narrator: It is about a half-hour later. Dani and her father have finished the dishes and are watching TV in the den. Her father has dozed off.

(The doorbell rings. Dani answers the door, and Matt, Kristen, Jamal, and Elena come in. The five head into Dani's bedroom. With the ransom note and the photo of Cassie in hand, Dani sits on the floor. The others gather in a loose circle around her as she puts the photo and ransom note in front of her so everyone can examine them.)

Dani: This is what we've got to work with, guys. This and a lot of questions. *(She holds up one finger.)* Question number one. Why did Mrs. Barr's house have so little furniture?

Matt: That's obvious—because they're so poor.

Dani: Wouldn't it have been smarter to kidnap a rich person's kid?

Elena: Crooks aren't always very bright. In fact, I'd guess they're pretty low in the IQ department if they turn to crime in the first place.

Dani: *(Smiling, she raises two fingers.)* Question number two. What did you notice about the clothes in Cassie's closet?

Kristen: They all looked old and way out of style.

Why do you think Dani takes the ransom note?

A Case of Being Yourself **105**

Matt:	Like I said about the furniture—they're poor, so maybe her mom can't afford to buy her new stuff.
Dani:	*(raising three fingers)* Question number three. What's with the other bedroom? It didn't look like anyone was using it to me.
Jamal:	And what about the tapes by Cassie's bed?
Kristen:	We're talking oldies. I mean, she didn't have anything current.
Dani:	And did anybody notice the book on the table?
Elena:	Yeah, I read *Bambi* when I was in kindergarten. *(furrows her brow)* What are you getting at, Dani?
Dani:	I think we'll know for sure in a minute. *(Dani gets up, takes a seat at her desk in front of her computer, and boots up the machine. The others get up and stand behind her, watching the screen.)*
Dani:	*(working the keyboard and gazing at the monitor)* My mom said Mrs. Barr came from Harper, Wisconsin, and that her husband died there in a boating accident last year. Let's get on the Internet and see if there are any articles about an accident involving a Mr. Barr in Harper, Wisconsin, last year. *(The kids huddle over Dani's computer, studying the screen, eager to see what Dani comes up with.)*
Dani:	*(a few moments later, excitedly)* There is no record of a man named Barr getting killed

	like that in the last twenty years anywhere in Wisconsin. But there *was* a series of unsolved kidnappings all over the state. Each time, the daughter of a widowed woman was the victim.
Elena:	Just like in this case! And now this creep's in our town doing the same thing!
Dani:	*(thinking)* That's true, but—
Matt:	*(impatiently)* Come on, Dani. You know who the guy is—tell us!
	(Instead of answering, Dani picks up the ransom note, the photo of Cassie, and the slip of paper with Cassie's height and weight written on it. She hands them to the others. The items go from person to person, and as they do, each kid's face lights up with sudden understanding.)
Dani:	See what I'm getting at?
All:	We sure do!
	(Dani picks up the phone and dials.)
Dani:	Hello, Mom?

SCENE 4

Narrator:	Mrs. Radek is driving to the Weatherby place in the patrol car. The kids are with her, chattering away about what they've figured out. A few minutes later, its lights out, the patrol car pulls to a stop not far from the house. A silhouetted figure is going in and out, from the house to the old pickup—now fully loaded again!

PREDICT

Stop reading. Can you solve this mystery? Who kidnapped Cassie Barr? Explain your answer.

Mrs. Radek: *(into the car radio handset)* It's all happening at the Weatherby place, folks. *(She laughs.)* You'd better get over here pretty quickly. I'll have the kidnapper in custody by the time you pull up.

Narrator: Mrs. Radek has all the kids get out of the squad car, then goes roaring off in the direction of the silhouetted figure, who is just now getting into the truck. The car screeches to a halt behind the truck, and Mrs. Radek jumps out with her weapon drawn. In seconds, she has the suspect handcuffed.

Mrs. Radek: Your kidnapping days are over!
(Sheriff Hodges and several other deputies arrive. All look very <u>perplexed</u> *to see Mrs. Barr in handcuffs.)*

Hodges: What do you think you're doing, Deputy Radek? Release that woman!

Mrs. Radek: She's the kidnapper, sheriff. *(She turns to the kids, who are now on the scene.)* Explain it to him, kids.

Jamal: Well, we first became suspicious when we realized it didn't make any sense for the kidnapper to go after Mrs. Barr's daughter. I mean, why not nab a rich person's kid?

Elena: Yeah, and then there was the fact that all of Mrs. Barr's stuff was still loaded in her pickup. After all, she'd supposedly moved in three days ago, so why not unpack her things—unless she wanted to be ready for a quick getaway.

perplexed: confused; puzzled

Matt:	Elena's right. Mrs. Barr wasn't planning on staying at the Weatherby place long. She never had the electricity turned on, and the water was still coming out rusty from the pipes. In fact, I'd be willing to bet she broke into the Weatherby place to set up her scam.
Kristen:	The thing that really got me was that all the clothes were at least twenty years out of style. And the cassettes were all really old— definitely *not* the kind of music kids like today. And why? Because the clothes and the music were Mrs. Barr's!
Matt:	I was confused by the fact that only one bedroom—Cassie's—was being used. But as it turns out, Mrs. Barr was using the room herself and only made it *look* like a teenage girl's room.
Elena:	But she must have been in a hurry, because she didn't even stop to think that a teenager would never be reading a book like *Bambi*!
Narrator:	Several news vans with <u>minicams</u> arrive on the scene.
Kristen:	We all noticed clues, things that weren't right, but it was Dani who put it all together.
Hodges:	*(slightly irritated)* Put *what* all together? *(He turns to Dani.)* Would you care to enlighten me, young lady?
Dani:	*(holding up the ransom note and the notebook paper on which she wrote Cassie's height and weight)* Well, I started to suspect Mrs. Barr

minicams: small, portable television cameras

when I saw this ransom note. Compare it to this piece of paper I got from Mrs. Barr's house. It looks like the same paper, and it has a coffee stain in the same place.

We all noticed clues, things that weren't right, but it was Dani who put it all together.

Hodges: So you're saying that the ransom note and this paper came from the same notebook, right?

Dani: Exactly. *(Dani smiles proudly.)* Next, we have the fact that Cassie was registered at school by mail—I checked with the school admissions office. Anyway, nobody I talked to has ever seen Cassie—not before she was supposedly kidnapped, anyway.

Hodges: What do you mean by that?

Dani: Well, I saw her after the kidnapping. *(She holds up the picture she took from Mrs. Barr.)* Look real close and you'll see who this is. *(Dani holds the photo in the beam of a squad car headlight. Hodges and several other deputies stare at it.)*

Hodges: Well, I'll be!

Mrs. Barr: *(handcuffed, looking to Hodges)* So, you finally get it, sheriff? *(laughs)* Well, it sure took you long enough!

Dani: The photo you're looking at is over twenty years old. I checked it at a photo shop. It's on a type of photo paper not made since when Mrs. Barr was a teenager—that's because it's a photograph of *her*!

Mrs. Radek: It's all a scam, sheriff. Our worried mother here is also our kidnapper. She sets the stage by pleading poverty, gets a loan from a bank, then gets out of town so she can set up her scam somewhere else.

Jamal: *(stifling a laugh)* While all the police surround the drop site, Mrs. Barr makes her getaway with the twenty grand!

Narrator: The minicam lights go on, flooding the night scene in bright white light. A reporter shoves a microphone at Sheriff Hodges.

Reporter: Apparently you've arrested a suspect, Sheriff Hodges. Please, sir, tell us how you did it.

Hodges: *(squinting into the camera)* Well, uh, actually, Deputy Radek made the arrest and, uh, she figured out what was really going on.
(The camera turns to Dani's mother. She's surrounded by the teenagers.)

Mrs. Radek: I *did* make the arrest. *(She beams at her daughter and the other kids.)* But as to figuring things out, the real credit goes to these young people.

Reporter: What exactly did they do?

Mrs. Radek:	I'll have a statement to make at a later time. *(She puts Mrs. Barr into the squad car.)* But right now I suggest you talk to my daughter.
Dani:	*(looks at Mrs. Barr, scowling in the back seat of the squad car, then back to the camera)* Well, I guess this woman fooled a lot of people. But there's one thing she didn't count on.
Reporter:	What's that?
Dani:	She remembered what it was like for *her* to be a teenager. But she didn't know much about what teenagers are like today.
Mrs. Barr:	*(growls at Dani)* I hate smart kids!
Mrs. Radek:	*(getting behind the wheel of the squad car)* Well, I'm very proud of *my* smart kid. *(Smiling, she starts the car.)* And now it's time to put you behind bars, Mrs. Barr!
Narrator:	The strobes go on as the siren sounds and the squad car pulls away.

A Case of
Being Yourself

▼ Learning from the Story

This play ended with Dani and her friends proving that Mrs. Barr was the kidnapper. But what if the play ended differently? Work with a small group to rewrite the ending of the play (from Scene 4 on). Prove that someone else was responsible for the kidnapping. Assign a number to each group.

Present the play to another class. Stop at the end of Scene 3. Ask your audience to select an ending—by picking a number out of a hat, by rolling a die, or by spinning a game-board spinner. Present the ending your audience selects. The ending could change each time you present the play!

▼ Putting It into Practice

Should you turn your mystery into a movie or into a play? If your story is full of action and takes place in many different locations, try a movie. If it is full of dialogue and takes place in one or two locations, try a play. Working with a partner, look over each page of your mystery. Decide which action or dialogue to keep and which to drop in the movie or play version. Circle scenes that need more action or more dialogue in order to work. With your cowriter, turn your story into a play or movie.

BY THE BOOK

SOme writers will dO anything—absOlutely anything—tO get their stOries published.

Melissa Winthrop had worked for the Knights on the Triple-J Ranch as long as Jason could remember. She did the cooking, cleaning, washing, and ironing. The woman was a writer, too—or at least she wanted to be one. Over the years, she had written half a dozen murder mysteries—none of which had been published. When Jason was just a little boy, Melissa, then a young woman, would always talk about how she was going to "make it big one day." But now Jason was sixteen and Melissa, in her forties, still had no publisher who had shown even the slightest interest in her work.

The woman's failure to publish, it seemed to Jason, had done something to her mind. The more her books were rejected, the more frantically she tackled her writing. Her small, private bedroom on the ranch was just below Jason's, and he would hear her pecking away at the typewriter at all hours of the night. The next day, the poor <u>obsessed</u> woman—often with circles under her eyes—would do her regular chores, always pestering whomever she could corner while she talked about her latest murder mystery.

obsessed: haunted; consumed by one thought

But the Triple-J was a working ranch. Jason, his two sisters, Janice and Janine, and his mom and dad put in long hours, and they had only a limited amount of time—and a limited amount of patience—for Melissa's endless <u>prattling</u> about her quest to be an author. Jason's dad made it clear to her that she was free to write all she wanted, and he wished her the best of luck, but she was not to let her writing in any way interfere with her work—or anybody else's work—at the ranch.

In a way, Jason felt sorry for Melissa. She had failed in her life's dream—and it was obviously making her crazy. She did her chores at a nervous pace; sometimes talking to herself, and now and then actually scolding herself for making a mistake of some kind. And more and more frequently, she began lashing out at Jason and the rest of his family over odd things, such as walking into a room when she didn't expect them, or walking up behind her too quietly.

Finally, Jason's parents threatened to fire her over her <u>outbursts</u>. She apologized, promised to control her temper, and begged them for another chance. Despite their doubts, they let her stay on.

Almost overnight, Melissa's outbursts stopped. In fact, little by little, a change came over the woman. Though still a bit strange in her ways, now, more often than not, she had a smile on her face, and her spirits seemed to have definitely picked up.

"I'm writing a new book," she told everyone, "and it's unlike anything I've ever done before. It's unlike anything anyone has ever done before."

prattling: talking in a foolish way; babbling

outbursts: violent expressions of one's feelings

PREDICT

Why is Melissa being so secretive about her new book?

manuscript: an unpublished book, usually in typewritten form

kneaded: mixed dough by pushing and pressing it

intently: with close concentration

The entire Knight family was happy to see Melissa in good spirits and tried to support her. But whenever anyone questioned her about the new book, an odd look appeared in her eye, and a funny little smile twisted her face.

Jason had read some of Melissa's other <u>manuscripts</u>, but she would not show this book to anyone. This book, unlike the others, she would hardly even speak about. She'd even change the subject if anyone asked her too many questions about it. It was as though the book, to Melissa, was some sort of weird, private secret.

"Come on, Melissa, what's it about?" asked Jason one wintry afternoon as the odd housekeeper worked in the kitchen baking Christmas cookies and cakes for the annual Triple-J Christmas party.

"It's very scary," she said, and that was all . . . except she added, "I named it after the Christmas carol 'Silent Night.' "

"That's the title?" asked Jason.

"Sort of," Melissa answered as she greased a pan.

Puzzled by Melissa's odd answer, Jason persisted in asking her what the book was about.

For a long while it seemed she wasn't going to answer. Then, finally, she said, "A murder—actually, several murders."

"Where does the novel take place?" Jason asked eagerly, glad he'd finally gotten her going.

Melissa <u>kneaded</u> some dough, gazed into space, and smiled. "It's not a novel. It's nonfiction, you might say." She stopped work for a moment and looked into Jason's eyes <u>intently</u>. "Did you know, Jason, that life imitates art, and that art, at the same time, imitates life? The two are all mixed up together."

A bit taken aback by the strange answer, Jason fell silent. He was about to get up and leave when Melissa suddenly broke into a wide grin. "For almost twenty years I've been writing," she said with a weird chuckle. "But now I've finally found the perfect story—a book that every publisher will want. No doubt about it, my boy. This one will be a guaranteed best-seller!"

"How come?" asked Jason. "How do you know?"

Melissa shrugged, went back to work, and began humming "Silent Night."

The following day, Christmas Eve, Melissa went into town with Jason's mother and sisters to do grocery shopping. Jason had no trouble picking the simple lock to Melissa's bedroom, and no trouble finding the mysterious manuscript—under the bed, where she kept all her other attempts at writing. But he was startled when he looked at the large stack of papers. Melissa had written the book in code!

The first sentence began SILENT OT TISH YORST. And there was another oddity. The book had a dedication on the second page, written in readable words. It said: "To Ana Gram, whose book will be the first and last word."

Jason glanced at his watch. He had only two hours before Melissa got back. Maybe he could break the code in that time and read—at least skim—through some of it.

Somehow, he was sure, the dedication was the key to the code. Ana Gram, though a name, is also a term for any word that could have its letters rearranged to make a new

Stop reading. Can you break this code? What does it mean?

word. The first and last word of Melissa's book was *listen,* an anagram for "silent." Using this as a base, he unraveled the code.

The hair stood up on the back of his neck as he read the decoded title: *Silent Knights.* He was horrified when he finally figured out the first line: *Listen to this story, this murder, written before it happened.*

After scanning about fifty pages, Jason knew all he needed to. He was just about to shove the manuscript back under the bed when he noticed something sticking out from under Melissa's mattress. It was a pistol! Now he was sure of Melissa's evil <u>intentions</u>. Leaving the pistol where it was, Jason ran off to where his dad was working in the barn. He explained what he had read and what *Silent Knights* was about. Amazed that the housekeeper could come up with such a horrific plot, Jason's father immediately called the state police.

When Jason's mom and sisters returned from shopping with Melissa, they were shocked to find state troopers waiting in the living room. Melissa stared fiery-eyed at Jason when she saw the manuscript of her book on the coffee table. She looked as if she were going to murder him with her eyes as one of the troopers handcuffed her.

"What's going on?" exclaimed Jason's mother.

Jason pointed to the manuscript. "The book that Melissa has been writing," he explained, "is about a horrible mass murder. It happens on Christmas Eve, which would be tonight. It happens on a ranch called the Triple-J. And

intentions: plans

the people killed are Janice, Janine, and Jason Knight—and their parents."

Janice turned to Melissa. "You were planning to murder us?" she asked, her voice shaking.

"So many of the books they sell these days are about true crimes," said Melissa, a faraway look in her eyes. "But mine would have been the best! Instead of being written after the murder, this one was written before. Famous!" she cried. "I would have been famous!"

Jason and his family watched as the troopers escorted Melissa from the house and out to the patrol car.

"It's so frightening—and sad," said Jason. "She planned a murder just to get a book published."

His dad put his arm around him. "And you, son, saved our lives by solving a murder that never happened."

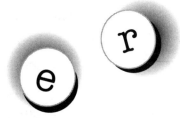

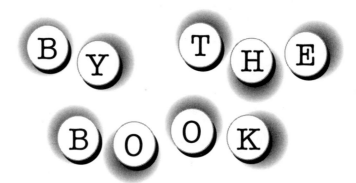

BY THE BOOK

▼ Learning from the Story

In "By the Book," Melissa wrote her whole book in code. She used anagrams, words with their letters scrambled. Working with several other students, brainstorm other types of codes a mystery writer could use. Then choose one and write a message in code. See if anyone else in class can solve it. Keep in mind that a good code should not be obvious. It should, however, be solvable by your readers.

▼ Putting It into Practice

You have the perfect setting and a cast of intriguing suspects. You've sprinkled clues throughout your mystery and gradually built up suspense. You think you're ready to put on your play or videotape your movie. Before you go any further, read your script out loud. Are you stumbling over words? Are your sentences so long that you can't remember what they're about? Does something sound corny? If so, time for another revision or rewrite! (Don't worry, even great playwrights and screenwriters rewrite their scripts—often many times.)